LIGHT YEARS

Books by Le Anne Schreiber

Midstream
Light Years

LIGHT YEARS

A memoir

Le Anne Schreiber

ANCHOR BOOKS
DOUBLEDAY
New York London Toronto Sydney Auckland

AN ANCHOR BOOK

PUBLISHED BY DOUBLEDAY

a division of Bantam Doubleday Dell Publishing Group, Inc.

1540 Broadway, New York, New York 10036

ANCHOR BOOKS, DOUBLEDAY, and the portrayal of an anchor
are trademarks of Doubleday, a division of Bantam Doubleday Dell
Publishing Group, Inc.

Light Years was originally published in hardcover by Lyons & Burford
in 1996. The Anchor Books edition is published by arrangement
with Lyons & Burford.

Library of Congress Cataloging-in-Publication Data

Schreiber, Le Anne, 1945–
Light years: a memoir / Le Anne Schreiber.
p.   cm.
1. Schreiber, Le Anne, 1945–   .   2. Ancram (N.Y.)—Social life
and customs.   3. Ancram (N.Y.)—Biography.   4. Country life—New
York (State)—Ancram.   I. Title.
[F129.A56S37   1997]
362.1'9699437'0092—dc21
[B]   97-21370
CIP

Text design and composition by Rohani Design, Edmonds, Washington.
All line drawings by Newton Schreiber.

"The Long Light" previously appeared in *Seven Days*, *The Independent*,
Uncommon Waters, *The Minneapolis Star Tribune*, and *The Little Book of Fishing*.

ISBN 0-385-48943-9

1   3   5   7   9   10   8   6   4   2

In memory of

BEATRICE SCHREIBER
NEWTON SCHREIBER
MICHAEL SCHREIBER

"Every man's condition is a solution
in hieroglyphic to those inquiries he would put.
He acts it as life before he apprehends it as truth."

— Ralph Waldo Emerson, from *Nature*

Contents

PART ONE: PARTICLES

The Long Light 3
The Glade 13
The Cat Tale 27
From Ashes 63

PART TWO: WAVES

Home 87
Names 109
Time 117
Territory 135

Acknowledgments 152

PART 1

PARTICLES

THE LONG LIGHT

⌐I WAS BORN CRAVING
summer, not for its warmth or colors or breezes. From the
womb, I wanted light, as much of it as my freshly opened
eyes could withstand. Since I was born in early August, I
was born satisfied—or at least I would like to think so. But
that first dark November, and every one since then, came
as a blow.

It's not that summer light is more beautiful than any
other season's; it's just that there's more of it. And make no
mistake, when it comes to light, more is better: ask any
Scandinavian; ask any sufferer of seasonal affective disor-
der; ask me. Being outdoors on a sunlit day is the only
self-justifying state of existence I know; it follows that being

indoors on sunlit days requires a lot of explaining, and what explanations I have been able to provide never suffice.

I was born knowing this, as I say, but it took me forty Novembers to arrange my life around the knowledge. Lacking independent wealth or the skills of a forest ranger (they spend too much time in the shade, anyway), it took some doing. The ten years I spent working in high-pay, low-light jobs helped, especially the thirty months I toiled in the windowless precincts of a newspaper sports department. After long fluorescent days, I was too depressed, too without desire, to spend the money I earned. So I toiled in darkness, saving for a sunny day.

On the brink of forty, single and self-propelled, I left offices behind. I climbed my way out from under the rock of Manhattan and moved to a rural hamlet in upstate New York, where I rented an old house to begin a new life. There I quickly discovered that getting in the vicinity of light isn't enough. You still have to figure out how to let it fall on you, which is not as easy as it sounds. There is simple basking, which has a lot to be said for it, but most of us lack the sublime temperament for prolonged, purposeless delight. It's the price we pay for not being lizards. There's sunbathing, which is just a hazardous form of napping, or one can simply do outdoors the things one routinely does indoors, like reading and dining. The trouble is, doing outdoors what one might better do indoors just leads to an indoor frame of mind. Who needs those page-flapping breezes, anyway?

Which brings me to fishing. I was resistant at first. I remembered summer vacations as a child, fishing with my father in a tippy aluminum rowboat on a lake in Wisconsin, snagging weeds and getting sunburned. We were after plump, tasty bass, but the usual reward for long periods of strictly enforced silence, broken only by an occasional racket of squeaky oarlocks, was the sight of a lean, mean, ugly, oily, snaggle-toothed fish called northern pike.

So when my tackle-bearing father visited me for Thanksgiving that first country fall, I politely thanked him for the hand-me-down rods and spared him my memories. Since legal fishing season was months away, there was no immediate need to confess my utter lack of interest. I looked attentive as he demonstrated his fly-casting skills in my snow-crusted backyard, and kept up pretenses by showing him my favorite spot on the stream whose steep bank formed the back border of my property.

In my early searches for idyllic basking sites, I had discovered a fallen sycamore whose double trunk spanned the stream from bank to bank, offering itself first as a cradle for my early, failed attempts at basking, later as seat and footrest for my contemplation of that failure. One light-filled afternoon, while pondering the difference between humans and lizards, I noticed a flash of silver in the water, which marked the beginning of my life as a fish watcher.

Nearly every day since then I had spent an hour or more sitting on my perch, staring into the water, watching dark shadows dart across the streambed at my approach and then slowly slink back as the creatures that cast them realized it was just the lady without a pole. By Thanksgiving, we had reached the point in our relationship where I could intentionally cast a shadow over their backs and they wouldn't bother to stir. Hooks were out of the question, I thought, as my father and I sidestepped together across the frosty log to the center of the stream. "Trout," he said, gazing into the swirling water with a wide smile of anticipation.

I had planned to keep my vigil on the sycamore all through the winter, not suspecting, of course, that within two weeks, the stream would be frozen solid from bank to bank. By Christmas, an opaque veil of ice stood between me and my fish, and nothing but spring could draw the veil back.

I waited. Those rods, stashed and forgotten in the rear of an upstairs closet, waited. Slowly, the afternoons began to lengthen. The ice thinned, turned transparent, and finally succumbed to the swollen urgency of the stream rushing beneath it. April came, and I resumed my perch on the sycamore log. May came, and I wanted to get into the water I was watching. What's the harm, I thought, in just pretending I'm fishing, strolling rod in hand through the sun-flecked stream, catching reflections? I could walk a stretch of the stream sufficiently distant from the sycamore that the fish gathered there would never have to see that suspicious long extension of my arm's shadow.

Some days I started downstream from the sycamore, at a shallow, fast-flowing stretch of the stream that suddenly stilled and deepened as it went round a bend and under a bridge. Other days I headed way upstream to a series of small falls and pools, always stopping well short of the sycamore. Taking tips from neighborhood boys, I fished first with live bait—minnows and worms. I was rewarded with nibbles, which seemed enough. I wasn't really fishing, after all, just playing a game of hide and seek with the trout, and I counted each quick tug as a tag.

I was getting to know the stream, certain stretches of it inch by inch. My sneakered feet searched the rocky streambed for secure footings while my eyes scanned the surface for signals. I took my cues from light and its interruptions, from shadows cast by overhanging trees or passing clouds or birds flying overhead, the darkening of the water over a submerged boulder or a deep hole in the streambed. Standing in light, I cast into darknesses where a trout might rest, cool, still, hidden, waiting for a morsel to tempt it into movement.

Then I caught my first fish, not on live bait, but on a twirling three-hooked lure that embedded itself, irretrievably, two hooks up and one down, deep in the throat of a very young, inexperienced, pink-finned brook trout. I watched it gasp and flap in my hand, watched its shimmering vibrancy turn dull and listless, then still and black. I had fallen in love with my light-filled game without ever believing it might come to this end. Nothing in my father's smile on the sycamore log that day contained a warning, nothing in my memory of our days on those Wisconsin lakes prepared me for this mangling. Catching, cleaning, eating, yes, but not this purposeless kill.

I called my father, and without blaming him outright for my sins, I let him know I wished he had never left those rods behind. He understood my distress but drew a different conclusion. The fault was not in fishing but in how one fished. For a different end, I needed a different means. I needed a fly rod, and if I would look in that closet again, I would see he had left me two —"both real honeys," a fiberglass and an "old split bamboo." He would tie me some flies on hooks too small to hurt even the most newly hatched fish. I could remove them from a fish lip with a flick of the wrist and release a trout, no sadder but wiser, to the stream. Should the hook be embedded more deeply, he had just the thing—a scissor-handled surgical clamp, the kind doctors use to remove stitches from humans.

Within three days I was back in the stream, unencumbered by minnow bucket or worm can or tackle box full of lures. I traveled light now, just a few bits of string and feather wrapped round tiny hooks, stuck in sponge and stuffed in my vest pocket. And a whippy, near-weightless rod. Since my goal now was to imitate what hovers just above the water, I raised my sights a notch, taking in the air and light as well as the water they stir and dapple. My focus lengthened, as did the summer afternoons, which now extended well into evening before I even considered leaving the stream. To my father's and my amazement, I began to catch respectable-sized trout almost immediately. With his long-distance help I mastered the art of quick release; the trick is patience, taking the time to play the fish out before reeling him in, so he arrives quietly in your hand, too tired to resist the flip of the wrist that will free him. We were in league with the trout, allies in their progress from season to season, training them to fend off the harsher assaults of worm danglers and hardware flingers.

At the end of long days in the stream, I called my father with news of the catch: A ten-inch brookie, a twelve-inch brown, the sight of a great blue heron lifting off at my approach, of an eight-point buck crossing the stream at the riffles, of a sleek-headed muskrat diving for the cover of his underwater door in the bank. I described whatever flitted above the stream, and he tied its likeness for me. Our phones seemed connected not by fiber optics but by the most delicately tapered of leaders, so sensitive that he felt the float of each fly, felt each slow swish of tail as the just-released trout steadied itself in the water before racing out of my loosely cupped hand.

He made my learning easy, but one thing I learned the hard way. "That's too bad," is all my father said when I told him I had broken the tip of my rod on a careless back cast into a tree branch. The next day, when I took the "old split bamboo" to the nearest tackle shop for repair, I was unprepared for the whistles of appreciation and dismay that greeted the sight of my broken rod. In my ignorance, I had chosen it over the fiberglass as the best rod for a beginner to bumble with. "Do you know what you've got here?" the shop owner asked, and I pretended that I had always known what I was just beginning to understand. He told me he knew a guy over in Massachusetts who used to repair split bamboo just for the love of it, but he might be out of business now, because hardly anybody who has a split-bamboo rod actually fishes with it anymore. They just hold on to them as investments.

When I told my father the guy in Massachusetts thought the rod could be repaired but it would never be whippy again, he said, "Well, I've caught a lot of good fish on fiberglass." For the next three trout seasons so did I. The phone and mail flowed between us like the stream, rising to its highest level in late spring and tapering off to a trickle in the fall. He sent me flies and I sent him photographs of my new favorite stretch of the stream; one time I even included a diagram showing the exact spots where I had seen the buck crossing, the heron lifting off, the big one that always gets away. Each year he planned a visit so we could enter the stream together, but each summer he was detained, first by my mother's illness, then by his own.

On my last visit to him, I saw that he kept those pictures at his bedside. Thumbworn at the corners, they still glistened at the center. One August morning, he asked if we could talk about a few things, "just in case." He said he would like a portion of his ashes to enter the stream, and I said I knew just where. No, not where the sycamore spanned the stream; the winter after my mother died, the sycamore had been pried loose from its mooring on the bank by the force of high water released during a rare January thaw. Without the fallen sycamore to slow and deepen the stream, there was nothing special to keep the fish there, and they had departed.

There was a better spot now, I told him, and, picking up a photograph, I pointed to the riffles where I had seen the buck highstep, head erect, across the stream and disappear into the woods. Anything that entered the stream there would flow downstream past all the spots marked on the diagram to the stretches I would explore next summer and the summer after that. He smiled at the idea, and that's all it was, an idea, "just in case." Then he asked me to go down to the basement, to the workshop where he tied flies and fixed whatever was broken, because there were some things down there he wanted me to have someday.

His work table was in order, cleared of projects for the first time in my memory. Sitting on the table was the wicker creel I had seen in pictures of him fishing as a young man. I looked closely this time, saw the well-oiled leather of the creel's shoulder strap and harness, its polished silver clasps. Next to the creel was a long oak case I had never seen before. I opened it and found five pristine sections of split-bamboo rod, with three different end sections of varying weights and whippiness.

It is spring now. The afternoons are beginning to linger. Rod and creel and ashes wait with me for summer, for the long light, when they will enter the stream at the riffles. Sometimes I wonder if the creel is his permission for me to keep what I catch. Right now, it seems more important that he taught me how to release. This summer I will carry the creel, empty, and bear the wicker weight of his absence. They say death comes as an invitation to light. I hope so. I would like to think of life as a progress from light to light.

THE GLADE

─W HEN I FIRST MOVED upstate
and rented a drafty old house in a tiny hamlet strung along a
bend in a stream, I did not think it was important for me to
own land. With the help of a rope tied round a tree trunk, I
could lower myself down the steep bank that formed the
edge of my backyard directly into the Taghkanic Creek.
Gazing out my car window as I drove the winding country
roads, I saw what seemed a lifetime's worth of creek-laced
woods and rolling meadows to explore. From certain hilltops
one could scan the breadth of the county from horizon to
horizon and count the visible habitations on one hand.
Owning a piece of the county would just keep me tethered
to one spot when I wanted to roam freely over all of it.

But after two years of pricking my jeans on barbed wire and reading wishfully between the lines of NO TRESPASSING signs (certainly, they don't mean me), I came to think differently. Ownership might not be important in the best of all possible worlds, but this was Columbia County, 1985, all its once-wild beauty claimed and staked, albeit in larger, more alluring packages than one can find in most parts of the civilized world. Clearly I needed a patch of my own, and in 1986, when I finally bought a house in the nearby village of Ancram, I got it. It wasn't much—just one sloping acre shaped like a blunt-tipped piece of pie being lifted from the pan—but it was unposted and all mine.

The narrower, front third of the acre was given over to house and lawn; the back two-thirds, though once tended, had been left to its own devices for at least fifteen years. During that time it had vegetated, which in no way means it had been inactive. I moved into my new house in July, when the larger portion of my acre was an impenetrable tangle of briar, staghorn sumac, thorny blackberry bushes, and wild honeysuckle, all festooned with miles of runaway grapevine. Poking up through the tangle, but tethered to it by long skeins of vine, were several tall trees—elms, maples, ashes, and black cherries bound like vertical Gullivers to the tenacious undergrowth.

My first thought was to bulldoze the jungle and start with fresh green lawn, perhaps accessorized with a few well-placed flower beds. My second thought, which came after a couple weeks of listening to the ceaseless drone of my neighbor's tractor mower, was to leave it alone, at least for the summer growing-and-mowing months. My third and best thought, which came in the fall, was to renovate. I would approach the jungle in the same spirit I had approached the house. I would try to respect its nature but feel free to make it congenial to the needs of its new caretaker. My first need was to enter it, which meant I would have to carve paths.

I bided my time until leafless November, when I could at least peer into the tangle and plot my entrance. I invited two friends and their machetes for lunch one day, and by sunset, which in November falls shortly after lunch, we had hacked our way in to the heart of the jungle. In the following days I kept working to turn our first dents into a meandering path which ended in a small clearing, that I envisioned as a large glade.

All winter I kept at it, enlarging my share of the turf, yanking thirty-foot lengths of choking grapevine out of strangled tree limbs, pruning back the crisscrossed arms of interlocking honeysuckle bushes, lopping off the brittle, spindly trunks of sumac trees at ground level. By spring I had my glade, a well-sculpted grassy oval about forty feet long and twenty-five feet across at its widest point; the honeysuckle-lined paths leading into and out of the glade were shaded by overhead arches of grapevine, just a few strands strategically spared to create green tunnels of filtered light. By late June, the palmlike fronds of an isolated stand of tall sumacs would provide morning shade to the eastern edge of the glade; to beat the afternoon heat, I strung a hammock between a lone, ancient apple tree and a towering white pine that defined its western boundary. It seemed my work was done.

The respite was brief. Within a month, the jungle had reasserted itself. Every cleared inch of the glade was knee-

deep in baby sumac. Newly sprouted branches of honeysuckle clasped sweet-smelling, sticky hands across the
bowered paths. The weight of the honeysuckles' berried new
growth lowered the boom of overhead grapevine to neck,
then chest, and finally to waist height. The grapevine itself
was, of course, not standing still but sending out new tendrils
that threatened to become anklecuffs if I stood (or, more
likely, crouched) in their vicinity for more than an instant.

I joined a summer-long battle, gaining and giving
ground. Armed with an expanded arsenal of pruning clippers and saws, I skirmished with the honeysuckle and
waged all-out war against the mighty grapevine. I traced the
path of deceptively dainty green tendrils back through a
series of forks, observing how the vine grew larger at each
juncture until, perhaps twenty yards later, it entered the
ground in shaggy-barked loops as thick as my legs. When
I sawed through the vine, it wept a clean, clear water that I
wanted to sip; weeks later, it still oozed, but the liquid had
thickened to a crystalline sap.

Meanwhile, I discovered that the staghorn sumac was
doing underground what the grapevine had done above
ground. Though each slender tree looked as if it had a life of
its own, just below ground they were united in a rhizomatic
conspiracy to take over my acre. Each sumac was connected
to the others by a shallow, horizontal network of thick
fleshy roots that sent up a dozen new recruits for every vet-
eran lost in battle. So days of pulling grapevines from their
treetop aeries alternated with days of tugging sumac roots
from their underground bunkers. Fortunately, by August the
pace of growth had slowed to a leisurely level, so that once-

a-week patrols were all that was needed. September came, and again I had a sculpted bower.

Then came October 4, 1987. The sun had set the previous day on the fiery reds and golds of a New England fall nearing an early, splendid peak. On the morning of the fourth, I was awakened by the sound of rifle fire. The bursts did not have quite the rat-a-tat-tat rapidity of semi-automatic weapons; it was more as if I had dreamed myself into the furious opening rounds of a major Civil War battle, woke, and found it true. Rising for a reality check, I looked out my bedroom window and saw an unpigmented blur, a cloud of un-color that blotted out sky and hill and road. A freak storm was blanketing the village with a foot of snow.

The weight of the wet snow accumulating not on bare winter branches but on all the landing surfaces offered by fully leaved trees was too great for even the sturdiest limbs to bear. Top limbs cracked first and fell onto lower limbs that crashed onto still lower limbs, which then joined in a tangled free fall until they hit ground. Sometimes the fall was broken by power lines, whose wires now crisscrossed the unpassable roads of the village.

While my eyes took in the wreckage around me, my ears registered the awesome extent of the devastation. The sound of rapid rifle fire continued for over an hour, then slowed to a loud crack every thirty seconds, then ninety seconds, then every few minutes. Finally a hush fell over the village, the kind of hush that must once have been natural to Ancram, in the time before cars, electricity, telephones, and running water, all of which we would do without until roads could be cleared and power restored.

When the silence had lasted long enough to suggest that one could step outside without risking decapitation, I undertook a survey of my acre. Several large limbs from a forty-foot maple were sprawled across my front yard. Behind the house, the largest limbs of a two-story-high lilac dangled upside down, hanging on to the bush by threads of bark while their leafy heads rested on the ground. The heads of younger, more sinewy branches were also bent to the ground, but unbroken, and showed signs of rebounding when I shook them free of their weight of snow.

The jungle was impenetrable again, its shrubbery mashed to half its normal height by the weight of snow and fallen tree limbs. No vestige of glade or paths remained in this upside-down world, where the toppled crowns of tall trees served as anchors for huge bowl-shaped root systems that jutted high into the air. By noon the sullen, vengeful gray sky that had taken a swipe at color was beginning to brighten. The temperature rose through the afternoon to 40 and 50 and 60, finally reaching 65 degrees under a clear blue sky. Leaves reappeared, wet and glistening, their reds and golds and purples heightened to a mad intensity by the backdrop of light-bouncing white. Although brought low, the foliage had held fast; the weight of snow that had wrenched branches from trunks had not been able to sever leaves from branches. I stepped through the wreckage like a giant, brushing hips and shoulders against the brilliant fallen treetops.

For a few brief hours that afternoon, I enjoyed the thrill of our anomaly—Ancram was part of a beautiful disaster area. The next morning, however, the town woke to the ugly

reality of yesterday's snow rising as today's water in base-
ments that had to be bailed without benefit of electricity.
Water oozed from refrigerators as well, though not from
faucets, because our well pumps would remain as silent as
our sump pumps and furnaces until power was restored. The
village lived by candlelight and wood stove for ten days, a
situation whose romantic possibilities were undermined by
the cresting smell of rotting food and unwashed bodies.
After four days, I got out of town.

When electricity returned, so did I, ready to undertake
the job of land reclamation. But I needed help. This was a job
for power tools, and out of a wise concern for my limbs as
well as my land, I owned none. Help was, of course, in short
supply, since every homeowner within a hundred miles faced
the same enormous task of cleanup. After a week of fruitless
searching for able bodies, I finally got lucky when I came
across a business card freshly tacked to the bulletin board of
the town's only store, named "The Little Store." One phone
call and I had secured the advertised services of "Landscaper La Femme," her chain saw and pick-up truck. I was a
bit concerned when she said she worked alone, but when
Landscaper La Femme (aka Deborah) pulled into my driveway the next day, I took one look and knew she was up to the
task. (She could have stopped traffic, if there were any in
Ancram, when she showed up for a Halloween party at the
local tavern a couple weeks later dressed as Wonderwoman,
tights-clad and caped, her long blonde hair bouncing with
each silver-booted stride of her long, lean legs.)

For two days, Deborah and I worked side by side. Well,
actually, I tried to keep a good ten feet between myself and

the chain saw, which Deborah kept in continuous swinging motion as if it were a bullwhip with teeth. I followed in her deafening wake, creating neat stacks of future firewood from the trunks and larger branches of former trees. Brush and severed treetops were hauled to an open area Deborah had cleared on the perimeter between woods and lawn. This, she suggested, would be a good burn site.

On the second afternoon, we created a pyre the size of a small log cabin and stuffed the equivalent of several balled and wadded Sunday *New York Times* into its interstices. After running through a three-pack of kitchen matches, we had succeeded in burning quite a bit of old news but nothing else. The wood was too wet and green to burn, but Debbie had a solution: gasoline, two gallons of it, which she splashed generously over the pile. We were within match-flicking distance of the pyre when the flicked match landed; a fireball whooshed thirty feet into the air with a roar so loud that fear fixed me to the intensely hot spot—one slight shift in the wind and I was kindling.

The wind did not shift, and the flames quickly subsided. Too quickly. Before the afternoon was out, Deborah had repeated her dousing and flicking technique several times, once when I was on top of the smoldering pile compacting it by stomps of my heavy, ash-coated boots. That moment, when the lit match landed at my feet, was the closest I've come to flying while awake.

Miraculous as it seems, we completed the job without injury, without even a scratch or a singeing. The price I paid for our recklessness was insomnia. The ashen remains of my acre's wreckage smoldered for three days; I kept vigil through the night by looking out my bedroom window as faint plumes of white smoke burst into imagined flames. Finally, the scorched ground turned cold, and a neighbor told me nothing would grow there for several years, not even the sumac that had so recently occupied the spot.

The rest of the winter brought nothing so dramatic as that early crushing storm. When spring arrived, nature continued the process of repair that Landscaper La Femme and I had started. The ancient apple tree, which had been so uprooted that it toppled onto its side, which I had saved from the chain saw so that it might feed deer and house birds over the winter, blossomed. Younger, more flexible trees that had been bowed to the ground but not broken sent up vertical shoots along the entire arc of their trunks; by midsummer one could walk under an archway of trees that had taken on the branching pattern of a menorah. The honeysuckle expanded its territory, taking advantage of every gap in the ranks of greenery. And despite my neighbor's warning about the sterility of scorched earth, the irrepressible sumac regrew to a height of six feet above the ashen rubble of our bonfire.

    The honeysuckle, the sumac, and I renewed our hostilities, but I entered the fray in a different spirit. I knew there was no war to be won, just an annual engagement with worthy adversaries whose tenacity I admired, even counted on, to survive my onslaughts. I had intended a limited, one-time intervention, as if paths and a glade could be carved out of a jungle once and for all, as if my acre, like the house it hosted, would sit tight for interior decoration. As if I were the character, and the acre merely a setting, not a protagonist, with purposes of its own.

Raised on sidewalks, I had not realized that a path must be walked every day to remain a path. Or else it becomes a faint trace and then disappears, swallowed utterly by wilder, steadier, more committed forces, their ranks closed tightly against the trespasser. Even a well-trod path does not rest quietly underfoot. I've learned that if you clear away a high growth, another, lower growth will arise, having finally found air and light enough to assert itself, and if you are patient, you might find something you like has presented itself. My paths, once paved with twigs from branches I had pruned, were covered for a time with a bright green creeper called moneywort, which hugged the earth more closely than grass and in summer offered up a sweet yellow flower to my feet.

The first strings of its dime-sized leaves appeared at the path entrance, in the gaps between stones I had harvested from my vegetable garden and placed there one season with grand ambitions for a cobblestoned path. After pushing a couple wheelbarrows of stones uphill to the mouth of the jungle and digging individual beds for each stone, I abandoned that scheme. I didn't realize I was issuing an invitation to the moneywort, which my newly acquired wildflower book told me is particularly well adapted to rock gardens. So what began as a vision of stone permanence became a seasonal green carpet that crept up the path toward the glade, taking three summers to arrive there. The next, drought-plagued summer, it disappeared.

In the glade, I let weeds grow for a season to see what they might become—perhaps a prickly nuisance called stingweed, perhaps a welcome splash of wildflower. The following spring I know better what tender growth to clear, what to leave. Brought by wind and birds, or sometimes just awakened by the sun from a long, shaded sleep through the midwifery of my pruning shears, wildflowers make surprise appearances at the edges of the clearing—black-eyed Susans, tall velvety mullein, glossy yellow buttercups, a single mauve coneflower—here one season, gone the next, despite my invitation to return. I've read that seeds can lay in wait for decades, even for centuries and millennia, until the right conditions arise for them to resume their growth. Disturb the soil, and you never know what you are resurrecting, what burying.

Both experience and booklearning strongly suggested that my ongoing efforts to shape the jungle would be matched by equal parts of serendipity and disaster. I came to enjoy that measure of unpredictability; it was what made my labors a kind of play for all seasons. I made many of my incursions in late fall and winter, when leaflessness exposed the architecture of shrubs and trees, and when a vast hillside of older woods beyond my acre was open to my exploring. If my acre showed what nature could do to a lawn left unmowed for fifteen or twenty years, the densely wooded hillside, like most New England woods, was testimony to what became of farmland left unplowed for fifty or sixty years.

Most of the trees—whether maple, oak, birch, wild cherry, or ash—had achieved a height of about forty feet on trunks of one-foot diameter. I have found only one tree that must have predated the time when these woods were fields. Late one March afternoon, when lengthening daylight allowed me to roam farther than usual, I was startled when the hush I walked in was shattered by a sudden, unidentifiable whooshing sound that was, oddly, both soft and thunderous. I walked through the woods toward the sound, which continued to build, until I finally saw its source—a flock of migrating birds, several hundred strong, lifting off in waves from their perches in a tree whose canopy of bare branches covered a span of fifty feet.

The flock had been taking a break in an oak with a trunk at least four times wider than any other tree I'd seen on the hillside. A toppled stone wall led up to and away from the oak, and remnants of a wire fence were embedded in its trunk—clear indications that this tree had been spared the ax to serve as a boundary marker. And yet, despite its hard-won girth, this lone survivor of the hillside's natural and human history was now in danger of succumbing to a force mightier than the ax—grapevine. The oak had been surrounded and ambushed by a regiment of ancient vines, whose attacks were being launched from enormous root systems located under the outer periphery of the tree's canopy. From there the vines stretched to the uppermost branches, several of which had been severed from the body of the tree but were held in place by a chokehold of vine.

I did what I could by hand that day to free the oak from its fate and returned many more times with pruning saw and clippers. I made the oak's survival my business, but I also quickly realized the hubris of my interventions in processes that so far precede me and will so inevitably outlast me. The near certainty of ultimate defeat in such efforts is probably what inspires the metaphors and mentality of military engagement, particularly when going hand to tendril with grapevine. But unless one is committed to the slash and burn of total victory, whose modern equivalent is power mowing and dozing, one is better off negotiating an early truce. Let me have paths, a glade, and the oak; do what you will with the rest.

After striking that bargain with my private jungle and the hillside beyond it, I wanted to undertake a somewhat more controlled and limited experiment; I wanted a proper garden. I envisioned a large perennial border as a buffer between lawn and jungle, a sort of flowery, peaceable DMZ where there might be daily patrols but no battles. But first I had to clear the site, and that meant bringing a bulldozer onto the acre for perhaps the first time in its history. I didn't like the idea of bulldozing, but I knew that creating a bed of tilled earth from this stony, root-clogged ground was beyond me and my hand tools. So I hired David Boice, who promised to be as gentle as his two-ton scooping, scraping, and clawing machines permitted. I had bought house and acre from his ninety-four-year-old grandmother and knew David cared about this parcel of land at least as much as I did.

After dislodging a small mountain of boulders and brush, David wielded his backhoe with the delicacy of a gourmand probing a lobster claw for its last sweet morsel. He left me a smooth, ever-so-slightly graded rectangle of earth, about fifty feet long and fifteen feet wide. It was perfect in form but odd in color—more mustard yellow than slate gray. Apparently the topsoil had been turned under, changing places with what I guess you might call the undersoil. No matter. I would restore the layers to their proper order by hand when it stopped raining.

A few days later, I walked up the grassy slope of back-yard with shovel and rake. The pressure of one foot on the shovel produced no results, so I jumped onto the shovel with both feet and landed flat on my back. A second jump and I broke the tip of the shovel. Apparently, when you take a very clayey soil and turn it under and then knock the wind out of it by rolling heavy equipment over it, you get something called hardpan, which is an organic form of cement. No matter. I would rent a power tiller from the local farm supply store.

Two days later I walked up the grassy slope lugging a gas-powered tiller, the country equivalent of a jackhammer. I found that if I held it in place for about ten minutes, the tiller could penetrate the ground to a depth of some six inches, creating a patch of finely ground yellow dirt the size and shape of a child's sand pail. Unfortunately, in the time it took to till a second pail-sized patch, the first patch rehardened. Apparently, under the slightest pressure, say the weight of a raindrop, ground-up yellow clay reverts to hardpan.

When I complained to David, he said not to worry—within a few years, decomposition and freeze-thaw cycles would aerate and soften the ground. Until then, there would be no garden, but in the meantime I could sow ryegrass, which would find a way to grow, much as weeds find a way to poke up through cracks in city sidewalks.

It had been five years since I first entered the jungle swinging a machete. In that time, I thought I had come to know my acre well. What I failed to take into consideration was that my efforts had been almost entirely aboveground. I knew my acre's surface, but not its depths.

THE CAT TALE

Act 1

⁓HE ARRIVED AS a stray. It
was January 1987, the winter after my mother died, and the
first of many seasons I would mark that way, by the deaths
they preceded, contained, or followed. It was a harsh month,
when the temperature routinely dipped below zero and the
ground was covered with a foot of ice-crusted snow. Not
even the most resourceful cat could have survived the extremity of that winter without human intervention.

I first heard about him from my neighbor Jodie, under
whose porch he had sought shelter, perhaps drawn by the
smell of her famous cooking and her fetching calico, Jolene.

Since I was new to town, alone and petless, Jodie thought she might make a match between me and the stray, but I wasn't interested. I was not, as they say, a cat person.

I didn't even catch sight of him for a couple weeks, and when I did make his acquaintance, I was not charmed. I was in the kitchen, roasting a chicken for weekend guests, when I heard a loud thump followed by insistent, high-decibel whining. Wiping the steam from the glass panel in the upper half of my kitchen door, I saw him spread-eagled a few inches from my face, his claws dug deeply into the mesh of the outer screen door. I marveled that he could hang by his toenails several feet off the ground and made a mental note to move storm doors to the top of my to-do list.

Our introduction would have ended right then if my houseguest Simone, who is French and cat-loving, hadn't walked into the kitchen. "Oh, my, my, what a wonderful-looking cat!" she exclaimed at the sight of blondish fur mashed against mesh. Sensing an advantage, the desperately clinging cat raised the volume on his whining, and Simone walked toward the door saying, "He must be hungry."

Entering the kitchen, the cat, ignoring me, began making circles round Simone's ankles, which prompted her to ask for the chicken neck. When I protested that I was using it to make stock for gravy, Simone fixed me with an accusing stare and said, *"Mon Dieu,* how cruel! Can't you see he is starving?" Since Simone does not usually speak and behave like a storybook Frenchwoman, this outburst only confirmed my suspicion that cats bring out the worst in people. Nonetheless, I yielded the chicken neck, which the cat seemed not to chew but inhale whole.

While he downed liver, kidney, and heart, Simone surveyed the cat and pronounced him a very fine animal—strong, healthy, intelligent, and affectionate. She didn't mention some of his more obvious traits—that he was large, dirty, smelly, carnivorous, and, to judge by his entrance, pushy. His light coat was so grimy that when I reached down to pet him at Simone's urging, my palm returned black and smelling like an NBA locker room. His head was full of lumps and scratches. The only source of immediate appeal was in his eyes, which were a beautiful translucent blue.

Those remarkable eyes were enough to win him fifteen minutes' sufferance in my house; then, just as Simone was starting to raise the larger shelter issue, the cat won my gratitude by voting with his paws. He went to the door and, standing on his hind legs with his right paw stretched almost to the doorknob, demanded out as vocally as he had demanded in.

His first unsolicited visit was also his last. Perhaps observing my house from his vantage under Jodie's porch, he somehow knew that his opportunity had come and gone with Simone and her overnight case.

It wasn't long, however, before Jodie renewed her importuning. The stray couldn't stay much longer under her porch because Jolene, who was something of a grand dowager, didn't want to keep his company; besides, another male cat was due to move in along with Jodie's boyfriend, Jimmy. The issue of Jimmy's Mr. Bill and his adjustment and search for happiness in a new home had apparently loomed large in their discussions of whether to live together, and Jodie seemed to fear that the stray's presence might daunt her man as well as his cat. After all, Jodie explained, Mr. Bill was "fixed" and the stray wasn't. I was so unfamiliar with cats that I had to ask Jodie how she knew the stray was unfixed. She drew my attention to the bowlegged strut of his hind legs, which seemed to hold a plump Georgia peach between them.

Jodie was a good neighbor, my first and best friend in town, and it was for her sake, not the cat's, that I agreed to let the stray set up winter quarters on my porch. On a clear but frigid afternoon in the third week of January, Jodie walked the hundred or so yards of curving country road between her house and mine, carrying a large cardboard box stuffed with an old army blanket and a half-empty box of Cat Chow; her ten-year-old son, Mercury, followed, carrying the cat, who had a wise dread of cars, past The Grog Shop (soon to be defunct) and The Little Store to my driveway. Jodie and Merc stayed for an hour, explaining the basics of cat care; when they left, the cat was sleeping contentedly on my porch. I quietly refilled his bowl and noticed that, with his body curled and compact, he seemed almost kittenish.

The next morning he was gone, but not far. Jodie called to say he was back under her porch. Thus began several weeks of my actively wooing the cat I didn't want, hoping for Jodie's sake that my efforts would succeed, hoping for my own that they wouldn't. In addition to the box, the blanket, and bowls of dry food and water, I added a plate of delectable canned food, first once and then twice a day. Jodie offered nothing, and still he returned to her porch every morning.

I studied Jodie's porch to see what it provided that mine didn't, and concluded the lure must be the scent of Jolene and a southern exposure that offered extra hours of the sun's warmth. I couldn't compete with Jolene, but I added occasional half hours of human company and central heating. I supervised him carefully during these times because I had been warned of the everlasting impression left upon furniture by spraying, an activity I understood to be a virtual ego-necessity for male cats.

It was during this period that the issue of naming first arose. It didn't seem right to keep calling him "the cat." In an immediate vicinity that included Jolene and would soon embrace Mr. Bill, the term was inappropriately unique and yet not particular enough. But I wasn't inclined to refer to him as "my cat," and for that very reason I was also reluctant to give him a name. A name would imply a more permanent connection than I intended. I understood my responsibility to this cat as seasonal; come spring, he was on his own.

Listening to the evening news one night, I hit upon a solution. I would call him Pussy M, an irreverent twist upon the court designation of the little girl who was the focus of a custody battle between her adoptive parents and the surrogate mother who had given birth to her. Unlike Baby M, who was shuttled between two mothers who desperately wanted her, Pussy M shuttled between two porch owners, neither of whom wanted him. More a designation than a name, Pussy M seemed to suit the temporary, custodial nature of our relationship.

As one sub-zero day followed the next, my blandishments began to have their effect. Pussy M's defections became fewer and of shorter duration. The temperature and a deep snow cover precluded much roaming, so mostly he slept. When I upgraded his housing by replacing the cardboard box with a picturesque wicker basket, Pussy M made sincere efforts to clean himself. Indoors, he was well-behaved, showing no inclination to scratch or spray or even to linger. A half hour now and then was all he seemed to want of domestic life. Really, he was no trouble.

Then one day, as I glanced down at him sleeping I saw something that startled and disturbed me. There was something in the bone structure of his sleeping face, in the strong flaring of cheekbone and brow, that recalled the refinement of a skeletally thin human face in repose. And when he opened his eyes I saw the exact blue of my mother's eyes, the translucence that had been the last living sign of her spirit.

My mother had died in October, and I was still in the grip of the magical thinking that too close a contact with death can inspire. There was indeed a resemblance of col-oration, and once I registered it, I couldn't stop seeing it, and seeing it, I couldn't stop my mind from making an alchemy of hues. But if this were reincarnation, it was born of bad karma. My mother hated cats. She justified this passion in the name of birds, but I suspected it had other roots, perhaps in a story my Aunt Veronica told. Like all the family stories, this one was very short, little more than bare fact whittled to a sharp point. She told how as small children on the farm, she and my mother had tried to please their mother once by taking her at her word when she said, "I wish somebody would drown those kittens."

Seventy years later, my mother had still turned red-faced with guilt whenever Veronica repeated that story, and now I felt the stabs of a double-edged guilt whenever I saw my mother's eyes in Pussy M's. It felt as if I had inherited the burden of my mother's unexpiated sin against cats, to which I added the sin of glimpsing her spirit in the eyes of a creature she dreaded. I am not talking about a consuming guilt, the kind one's rational mind gets behind and fans into flame; this guilt was more like the smoldering of ashes not quite extinguished by the wet blanket of consciousness.

There was a flare-up in early March, while I was enjoying a two-week vacation with a friend on St. Croix. By day, I floated face down watching pairs of sea turtles disport through turquoise waters lit by the Caribbean sun. By night I dreamed of Pussy M in his basket on a frosty porch, alone and forlorn under the cold, uncaring gaze of a winter moon. Finally I dreamed that a despairing Pussy M was perched on the edge of a snow-covered roof, preparing to leap off The Grog Shop to his death. It was a disturbingly vivid dream, the kind that upon waking still feels true, premonitory if not clairvoyant. The fact that the dream was ridiculous—both in its outline and particulars—didn't matter. However unlikely cat suicide, especially by means of a fifteen-foot plunge into a cushion of deep snow, I remained convinced that Pussy M was in danger. And I felt terrible.

As soon as I returned to Ancram, I called the local veterinary hospital to ask what needed to be done before letting a stray take up residence in my home. "Have you fed him?" the vet asked. To my yes, he responded, "Well, that was your first mistake." He advised me against formal adoption, saying that a male cat who had reached adulthood without being fixed would not make a good house pet. Even if he were neutered now, he would probably cling to old habits of roaming, fighting, and spraying.

While I was weighing the vet's advice, Pussy M took action. With the snow cover reduced to a damp few inches, he was able and apparently willing to fend for himself. He began disappearing from my porch, first for entire days and then for batches of days. Technically, it was spring; our contract had run its course. And yet I found myself unwilling to sign the release. My spirits rose and fell each morning not with the temperature, the usual spring index of my mood, but with the sight of a vacant or occupied wicker basket.

In early April, he pushed it too far. After six consecutive days of staring glumly at an empty basket, I got angry—at Pussy M for being an ingrate, and at myself for letting the comings and goings of a stray cat stir feelings of loss and recovery. As far as I was concerned, Pussy M was history. On day seven, I removed the basket from the porch. On day ten I stopped counting.

A few days later, while waiting at the counter in The Little Store, I looked at the front page of the local weekly newspaper and was transfixed. There, taking up half the tabloid's front page below the fold, was a grainy black-and-white picture of a cat behind bars, with an arrow shot through its body from shoulder to shoulder. Impaled and bloody, the cat was sitting upright and looking straight out through the cage bars, his eyes wide open in seeming accusation or appeal or recognition, the seeming, of course, depending on the beholder.

I walked the short distance home from the store, staring at the picture the whole way. Staring, but not thinking. I was too stunned by the freakish horror of the photograph to contemplate the possibility that this was Pussy M. But when the thought struck, it hit with the wrenching force of a dreaded certainty. Despite the graininess of the printed photo, one could see this cat had a light coat and light eyes, and the caption indicated "the male stray" had been found hiding in a storage barn not far from my home. I was certain it was Pussy M, and I was equally certain that the switchboard at Copake Veterinary Hospital was being flooded with calls from people who wanted to give him a better next life.

I called the hospital immediately to press my claim, which, though not unassailable, was probably stronger than anyone else's to Pussy M, whom I decided not to refer to publicly by that name lest it diminish my stature as a prospective cat parent. I simply said that I thought I knew the cat in the paper, that he was a neighborhood stray I had fed over the winter, and that I had recently called this very veterinary hospital about adopting him. To confirm identification, I asked the vet if his (the cat's) eyes were blue, and I was amazed when he said he hadn't noticed their color. He suggested I come in and take a look to make sure this was the cat I knew and wanted. He assured me there was no imminent danger of the cat going anywhere; despite my fears, no one else had expressed a desire for the cat with an arrow in him.

Ten minutes later I was ushered through swinging doors into a bedlam of barking dogs and one cat. As soon as the cat saw me, he started crying and butting his head against the bars of his cage. My first, outraged thought was, how could anyone not notice those beautiful blue eyes? My second thought was, how could I expect anyone to see blue when it was so upstaged by red? Blood red. Pussy M was a mess. He seemed half the size of the cat I last fed two weeks earlier. His emaciation was exaggerated by two shaved circles about six inches in diameter on each side of his body. The bull's-eyes of these white circles were two open red wounds the size of a half-dollar.

Despite the sorriness of the spectacle he made, Pussy M seemed oblivious to his wounds. The volume of his cries and the force of his head banging suggested there was plenty of strength left in his scrawny body. Insofar as I could read his meaning, he was saying, "Get me out of here!"

When I asked how soon I could take the cat home, the vet looked astounded and suggested I wait a couple weeks to give the wounds time to start closing. The vet would continue to give him antibiotics and, if I wished, "fix" him. After that, the cat—and his medical bills—would be all mine. In the meantime, I could visit however often I wanted.

With that deal struck, I explained the situation as best I could to Pussy M and steeled myself to leave him amidst the clamor of barking dogs. When I passed the receptionist on my way out, she said she would be keeping a medical record on the cat and needed a name for him. It came to me at once. "Sebastian," I said. The cat had practically named himself, after St. Sebastian, the early Christian martyr upon whose arrow-stricken body Renaissance painters so often mounted the head of a gorgeous blue-eyed blond.

Act 2

The cat I brought home in late April was a very different animal from the stray who had come to town in early January.

A farewell shampoo by the hospital staff had done wonders for his coat, transforming greasy dishwater blondness to pure glistening cornsilk. Weight loss had made him slender, and the vet's scalpel had pared his peach to something more resembling a walnut. Peachiness resided now in the fuzz growing on his shaved shoulders and in the healing, pit-sized wounds at their center. Temperamentally, Sebastian seemed tamed, or at least sobered, by the experience of being shot, starved, caged, and castrated.

Before handing him over, the vet assured me a complete recovery was likely since the arrow had not pierced any vital organs. The greatest danger now was infection, which I could minimize by making sure Sebastian's open wounds stayed clean. That meant keeping him indoors until the wounds were completely closed, which the vet guessed would take three or four more weeks. Outdoors, his visibly diminished state would also make him a tempting target for other animals. Sebastian, who sat quietly on a gleaming stainless steel table while the vet spoke, appeared to be listening attentively. A couple times, he nodded.

During the previous two weeks of frequent hospital visits, I had gotten into the habit of talking to Sebastian not only as if he were a human, but as if he were an adult. Although his responses were limited to head butting and a narrow range of cries, varying mostly in their volume, I assumed he understood that we now had a committed relationship. Many details of our living arrangements would have to be worked out, of course, but I felt sure that Sebastian, unbound, would have a much expanded repertoire of signals to communicate his point of view.

During the drive from the hospital, Sebastian crouched on a rear floor mat and whined piteously. I explained that we were headed home, where there were no cages, and he would be free to roam at will from room to room. That quieted him. Once inside the house, he took a leisurely stroll around the living room, pausing here and there to sniff, paying particular attention to table legs. Then he went to the front door, sat down, and fixed his gaze upward on the doorknob. I redirected his attention to the bathroom, where a new litter box had been installed, and the kitchen, where bowls of water and tuna-flavored crunchies awaited his inspection. He lapped a little, crunched a little, and then he went to the front door, sat down, and fixed his gaze upward on the doorknob.

I reminded him of what the doctor had said about staying indoors. He placed his right paw on the door and looked expectantly at me with his haunting blue eyes. I said, "Forget it, Sebastian, you're not going out." He stretched his right paw closer to the doorknob and let out a loud cry of protest. I left him there and went about my business, refusing to enter into a more prolonged discussion of the matter.

For three days, Sebastian held his ground at the front door, leaving his station only for occasional mad dashes to the back door or to the side door when he caught me trying to sneak in or out of the house. Food, water, litter box—all went unvisited. Sebastian wanted his freedom, and he wanted it *now*. That was the message of his unremitting howls and cries, the non-negotiable demand with which he met my every attempt to reason with him. As irritated as I was by his behavior, I did admire his resolute adherence to the high road of nonviolent protest. He never once resorted

to clawing or spraying or any other form of destructiveness
that might have won him a quick and permanent release.

On the fourth day, I cracked. I stopped trying to reason
with him and tried instead to rethink my position. However
much I might fancy myself Sebastian's savior, it was clear he
regarded me as his jailer. The fact that I ran a plush jail, several well-appointed rooms rather than the two-foot cube of
his recent past, apparently didn't make the slightest difference. Sebastian wasn't signing any social contract without an
open door clause. And if those were his terms, what right did
I have to confine him against his will? The concept of *in loco
parentis* didn't really apply here. Sebastian wasn't a kitten; he
had seen enough of life to make an informed decision about
the merits of contact with humans.

The ACLU would no doubt side with him, and so did
I in principle. But did he really understand that indoor living
for the next few weeks might be critical to his survival?
Before I could get too deeply into consideration of a cat's
right to die, I decided upon a compromise. Supervised out-
ings. I would let him out if he would promise to stay in the
backyard where I could see him. Promises were necessary,
because the yard was unfenced, and escape into nearby
woods would be easy. Interpreting an alert look in his eyes
as assent, I went to the back door and held it wide open.

I took the fact that Sebastian walked rather than dashed
out the door as a good sign. He took his time sniffing around
the deck, then began walking slowly up the steep slope of
lawn that leads to the densely wooded area of my property.
Halfway up the slope, he stopped to lie down in a pool of
delectable spring sun. I watched him from the deck for a few

minutes and then moved to join him. As soon as I started up the slope, he rose and headed uphill, which brought him closer to the woods. When I stopped, he stopped. It was clear that he wanted to keep at least ten yards between us, and that if I sprinted to close the gap, he would outrun me, probably to the safety of woods.

That sinking feeling settled into my stomach, followed shortly by a chest-rattling blast of self-contempt. I had made a mistake, a stupid mistake, in expecting this animal to co-operate in its own captivity. But there was no time for re-crimination. If I were to redeem the situation, I had to keep a cool head and try to outmaneuver him.

With veiled intention, I walked casually up the slope. Sebastian, with equal nonchalance, sauntered toward the woods. I hoped he would choose one of the footpaths I had hacked through the dense, thorny underbrush, but, no, he chose a route that admitted nothing taller than eighteen inches. I had no choice but to use my hand-hewn paths, hoping to intercept him at some later point. We each feigned indifference to the other's movements, but occa-sionally I would crouch low to catch a glimpse of blond fur moving through gaps in the green. Whenever he spotted me, he would stop in his tracks and feign a sudden, intense interest in grooming himself. Wily, patient, loath to let me know his next move, he must, I thought, have a specific des-tination in mind.

After ten minutes of stop-and-go stalking, I decided to take a gamble. He appeared to be headed in the general direction of the barn in which he had been found hiding with the arrow shot through him. I backtracked, loudly, to make Sebastian think I had given up pursuit, then hurried along the shortest human route—across two yards and a road—to the barn, which was situated in a clearing. I hid behind the barn and waited until, sure enough, I saw Sebastian emerge cautiously from the woods and, after looking both ways, run across the road, unsuspecting, toward my clutches. As he paused in the barn's open doorway, I pounced. I walked home with Sebastian gripped firmly in my arms. He did not struggle, and when I let him down on the kitchen floor, he went straight to his food bowl and put away his first meal in four days.

Our aborted outing had a certain bracing effect on our relationship. The pangs of guilt I had felt when it seemed Sebastian might elude the care he clearly needed settled an issue for me. Until he was healed, I was the boss. I would be a benevolent but firm despot. I would try to keep a tight lid on my anthropomorphic impulses, and I would try to banish magical thinking altogether.

This last resolve was not as simple as it might seem. It was easy enough, of course, to remind myself that Sebastian was a cat, that blue eyes notwithstanding, he was not my mother—in any of her incarnations. But the bizarre twist of this animal's fate had raised certain parallels to such a level of grotesque literalness that they became laughable—and inescapable. Wounds, weight loss, hospital visits, prescription medicine, danger of infection, the worry, care, responsibility: all were familiar, all evoked memories so recent it took little to reanimate them, all inspired a feeling of re-enactment. The resemblances were not of character but of plot.

What I needed to keep in mind was that this was Sebastian's Act Two. There was still a good chance that he was weaving a comic subplot into my life. There was, after all, no reason to believe my efforts in his behalf would be fruitless. Rather than deny the parallels, I should just relax and wait for the story lines to diverge. Sebastian was, if anything, my best prospect for a happy ending.

Sebastian was also my ticket to an acceptable identity within the village of Ancram, where "newcomers" remain newcomers for two generations, at which point they achieve the status of "relative newcomers." Since my arrival the previous summer, I had been known around town as "the lady who bought Mary Jane's house." And since Mary Jane had preceded me in Ancram by ninety-four years, there was an unavoidable undertone to the phrase, as if it were a euphemism for "dispossessor." So I was pleased to discover that Sebastian's front-page notoriety had the secondary effect of repositioning me within the community. He was now commonly referred to as "the cat with the arrow" and I, of course, had become "the lady with the cat with the arrow."

At the post office and The Little Store, my exchanges were no longer limited to the weather. Old-timers and newcomers alike wanted to know how the cat with the arrow was doing. It seemed my social standing was hostage to Sebastian's fortune. I couldn't take any more chances. I certainly didn't want to be known as "the lady who as good as killed the cat with the arrow."

Fortunately, my firmness soon had the desired effect on Sebastian. He gave up his vigil at the front door, and devoted himself to sleeping, eating, and healing. To my surprise, he offered no resistance to my daily washing of his wounds, in fact, he enjoyed my ministrations, hopping eagerly onto the kitchen chair that served as my examining table as soon as he saw the brown bottle of hydrogen peroxide in my hand. As the days passed, I was more than a little gratified to see the arrow holes steadily diminish from the size of peach pit to plum pit to olive pit. Whenever I left the house, he would, if awake, rush to join me, but it was with hope, not insistence, in his eyes, and he accepted my "no" as final.

It was during this time that we established some basic house rules. Sebastian could sit on any surface a human did, like sofas and chairs, but not on surfaces where humans didn't, like tables and kitchen countertops. That covered most of the household bases, except for beds (no) and toilet seats (maybe). Dinner at five. Snacks available at all hours. No scratching, spraying, or begging for human table scraps. Sebastian was a quick study, and as soon as he grasped a rule, he abided by it.

Within a short period of time, he was so genial and cooperative, even gentlemanly, indoors that I felt it was nearing the time to let him outdoors. His wounds were closed, and we were approaching Memorial Day weekend, when the frequent comings and goings of houseguests would make door monitoring almost impossible.

Two days before guests were due to arrive, I let Sebastian out. Succumbing to the pull of habit, he followed the pattern set by his first outing: deck-sniffing, slope-climbing, a rest, and then into the woods. As before, he signaled his dislike of my hovering and stalking by various means, including crawling beyond my reach under thickets and hunkering down to wait me out. Since my powers of surveillance were more limited than his will to elude me, I decided to trust him to return on his own. Three suspenseful hours later, my trust was rewarded.

From that day on, Sebastian was virtually free to come and go as he pleased; all he needed was someone to open the door for him. This last vestige of confinement apparently bothered him, however, and so he made sure it bothered me as well—about twenty times an hour. In, he wanted out. Out, he wanted in. That first weekend, guests eased the burden, particularly Simone, visiting for the first time since January, who was certain Sebastian remembered her, and who was further ingratiated when he submitted peacefully to sessions of shiatsu and paw reflexology. "I think it helped him, I really do," Simone said as she graciously ushered Sebastian to the door.

Alone again after the guests' departure, I began to feel like a cat valet. Since there was seldom an immediate motive for his frequent ins and outs, and since Sebastian was not otherwise given to neurotic behavior, I concluded this was his way of lobbying for a cat door. It was telling, I guess, that I didn't even recognize this as a strange thought. Did I think he had been browsing through the 1/16th-page ads in the back of my magazines? Whatever the source of his presumed desire, I was not going to be able to indulge it. Convenient as a cat door might be for both of us, I was far too house-proud to cut holes in my recently refinished hundred-year-old oak doors.

While talking on the phone with my father one day, I happened to mention this hitch in my relationship with Sebastian. He had been following the cat's progress closely and, like me, was eager to have a part in the story of Sebastian's return to health and happiness. Not long afterward, UPS delivered the fruit of his ingenuity—a cat window, custom-made by a man with too much time on his hands. My father had taken an ancient, industrial-strength window fan, removed the fan from its metal frame, and in the resulting circular opening constructed a swinging door of heavy rubber, elaborately hinged and weighted so it would close tightly against cold air but gently against a lingering cat tail.

Within minutes, I had installed the device in a window that opened onto the front porch; from inside the house, I demonstrated its purpose to Sebastian by pushing the swinging door open and placing a handful of crunchies on the exterior windowsill. He leaped onto the interior sill, stuck his head through the opening to get the crunchies, and gathered his good fortune in one sniff of sweet summer air. Hence forward, his departures and arrivals would be announced by the heavy thump of his landings on either porch or living room floors.

That cat window made all the difference. Although still a provider, I was no longer Sebastian's keeper, and this change in roles made it possible for us to become, well, friends. Indoors, Sebastian spent long hours happily curled at my side as I read or watched TV. For reasons no doubt shrouded in the mists of his unstoried kittenhood, he did not purr his contentment, but the corners of his mouth curled upward in an unmistakable smile. Outdoors, he no longer tried to shake me off his trail. We took long walks together in the woods and soon developed a repertoire of games. I might, for instance, select a tree for him to climb and signal my choice by tapping on its trunk. After sharpening his claws on bark, he'd charge straight up the tree and then let me guide him through a maze of forking branches by pointing to whatever tine of limb I wanted him to follow.

More often, though, we simply pooled our skills at tracking—our goal being a sighting, not a kill. His greatest interest was in rabbits and large game birds like pheasant and wild turkey, but their tracks often led to paths where I could not follow. I, in turn, tried to interest Sebastian in deer. Since his forte was catching scents (mine was deciphering prints), I simply showed a keen interest in deer scat, and he got the point at once. He would rush ahead of me on trails and sit sentinel at choice piles until I arrived to check out the freshness of his find. Once I saw Sebastian nearly trampled by a doe, frantic to reach a fawn as spellbound by Sebastian as he was by her.

Many hours of Sebastian's days (and nights) were, of course, spent alone in the woods, and so it became necessary to find a way to summon him home. Since I didn't like the idea of hollering his name at the top of my lungs, I developed a language of whistles. It began with the standard two-note whistle, the whistle of basic business, signaling I had some practical reason for wanting Sebastian to show himself, i.e., to get fed, to say hello or good-bye to guests, to show me he was still alive. It wasn't long, however, before I felt the need for a less peremptory whistle, one that was more invitation than command, a whistle that said, for instance, "Hey, Sebastian, would you like to take a walk in the woods with me?" Early one evening, when I wanted to signal exactly that, I impulsively whistled the first bar of the

Marseillaise, and Sebastian came running with a jauntiness
of stride that suggested he understood my tone perfectly.
And so we had our "let's play" signal.

Eventually I developed a third whistle. It was a long,
plaintive single note, seldom sounded, that was meant to say
"ple-e-e-ase." It was an honest whistle, indicating that I
wanted Sebastian to come to me but there was nothing in it
for him—no food, no play; I just wanted the comfort of his
company. Sebastian responded to the summons of all three
whistles, but this third whistle was the only one he answered
with a sound of his own. Whether I'd roused him from sleep
or the hunt, I would hear Sebastian crashing through brush
emitting an urgent, anguished cry that sounded for all the
world like, "I'm coming! I'm coming!"

Act 3

By the end of the summer, Sebastian and I were such boon
companions that I hated the idea of becoming his jailer
again, but he was developing repeated infections at the sites
of his entrance and exit wounds, and a new vet was recom-
mending surgery. Rebecca had been interviewing for a
position at the animal hospital the day the "cat with the
arrow" was brought in, and now that she was on staff, she
was eager to treat him. Without criticizing her colleagues,
she nonetheless implied that half-dead strays do not receive
the most thorough attention, particularly in rural practices
devoted primarily to horses and cows. Now, however, with
an owner and a vet avid for cure, we could lavish upon
Sebastian the miracles of modern veterinary medicine.

Rebecca took X rays, which showed that Sebastian had a hollow channel, the diameter of an arrow, running though his body from shoulder to shoulder. He must have been shot, she concluded, several days before he was found in the barn, long enough for scar tissue to have formed around the arrow. That would account for the channel left when the arrow was removed—a procedure, I now learned, performed by Sebastian himself. Someone on the hospital staff, bothered by the noisy clattering of arrow against cage bars, had snipped off the protruding front half of the shaft. With the tip gone, Sebastian was able to extract the rest by twisting his neck around, grasping the feathered end in his teeth, and pulling.

The X rays also showed a notch in Sebastian's right shoulder blade, and Rebecca guessed that bone fragments might be trapped in the channel, traveling from one end to the other, causing the recurrent infections. Her plan was simple: reopen Sebastian's wounds surgically, flush out the channel, and sew him back up, clean as a whistle. If her hunch about the bone chips proved correct, this intervention should put an end to the infections.

And so, early in October, I brought home a cat shaved half bald again and held together by two six-inch runs of large black stitches. Until the incisions healed, he was supposed to stay indoors. "That won't be a problem, will it?" Rebecca asked.

She should have been there in the middle of the next night, when I was awakened at 3:00 A.M. by a series of loud, thwacking noises. I hurried downstairs to find that Sebastian, in apparent determination to find his cat door, had gone from window to window, launching each of my

pricey, spring-loaded linen window shades like rockets toward the ceiling. Close inspection revealed no tears or claw marks in the shades, which meant he had sprung them by pulling on the small brass rings attached for that purpose. Could a cat that smart think I was dumb enough to hide his cat door behind anything so pregnable as a cloth shade? Or was he just firing a warning salvo?

The threat of destruction was not idle. As if mounting a systematic campaign, Sebastian shredded the silence that he knew was my most valued household possession. This time, he did not sit in quiet vigil at the front door, but went from room to room, from door to door, and from window to window, howling as loudly and for as long as he could before exhausting his poor, bald, sliced, stitch-riddled body. His wailing drove me out of the house by day, and by night I slept with pillows over as well as under my head.

I never relented, but in a moment of relaxed vigilance Sebastian managed to escape out the back door. With me in panicked pursuit, he ran full speed toward an ancient lilac in the backyard, leaped several feet into the air, and swung, trapeze-style, by his front paws from a horizontal branch, popping every one of his stitches. I snatched him up and, pressing his profusely bleeding body against me to staunch the flow, ran to the car, where I swaddled him tightly in a beach towel before speeding to the vet's. There Rebecca calmly stapled Sebastian together and handed him back to me with a warning not to "let" him out again.

Home, he resumed his howling. The three weeks of his recuperation were so terrible a trial that I seriously considered putting him up for adoption. At times I felt murderous rage toward the animal I was committed to saving. And it was clear that, to Sebastian's way of thinking, I was the enemy. I tried not to take his behavior personally, knowing by now that freedom to roam was as essential to his nature as the need for food and water. But I did not like living with enmity, personal or impersonal.

In November, when I finally opened the door for a freshly reminted Sebastian, I thought I might never see him again. What happened instead was that I let out a lion, and several hours later, let in a lamb. There would be no hard feelings on his side, as long as I kept a cat door in the window. I was slower to forgive, but not by much. I wanted to reap the reward of that happy ending, and I wanted his companionship for the short days and long nights of the winter ahead.

We resumed our daily walks in the woods, ranging farther afield now that autumn had opened new paths by thinning the undergrowth. The freak snowstorm on October 4 did more than the usual fall thinning; it virtually leveled the distinction between the upper and lower stories of the woods. Now, after a month of gusting winds, twenty-foot lengths of elm, maple, and beech not only littered the ground, haphazardly layered like pick-up sticks; they dangled precariously overhead, hanging by only a few threads of tenacious bark; or, fully severed from their trunks, they rocked in the crooks of other trees where they had been snagged on their fall to the ground.

Sebastian's progress through this mayhem was nimble and surefooted; a world of daunting verticals had been transformed into an inviting lattice of horizontals, a nature-made jungle gym for his effortless climbing. I, however, who in

September had marched confidently at the head of our pro-
cession, now brought up the rear, slow and stumbling. This
reversal had consequences. In the woods our relationship
was as profoundly altered as the terrain. Emboldened by my
newly exposed incompetence, Sebastian asserted his domi-
nance. We still played by my rules at home, but in the woods
he was top cat, and I was not to cross his path. When he
stopped to sniff the wind, I was expected to stand still until
he had sized up the situation. If I even shifted my position,
he would rear up on his hind legs and swat me. He was not
idly overbearing; he was trying to teach me how to survive.

There was a change in our behavior indoors as well.
Shortly after Thanksgiving, I learned that my father had a
form of cancer so rare that most oncologists had never seen
a case. There were treatments, but no cure, and although he
might live another ten years, he might not. Many nights that
winter, this knowledge pinned me in place on the couch, my
body still, my mind racing, mostly in frantic circles of
remembrance and projection. Often, when I was in this
state, whose only outward signs were my motionless sitting
and blank-eyed staring, Sebastian would climb unbidden
onto my lap; then he would stretch his long body out
against my chest, extending his arms on each side of my
head so that a paw grasped each shoulder. I don't know
where he learned how to hug; perhaps it was instinct.
However he came by this gesture, it was inspired in its timing and in its effect.

Indoors and out, we were inseparable that winter,
except for my occasional weeklong trips to my father's home
in Minnesota, or to my brother's home in Pennsylvania,

where we hoped my father might be persuaded to move. My brother was a doctor, chief of staff at his hospital, and so he could surround my father with dedicated care as well as grandchildren. As long as he could manage by himself, though, my father preferred the familiarity and independence of his own routines.

Upon my returns, Sebastian would greet me with an outburst of noisy reproach. Under normal circumstances, he spoke seldom, and his tonal variations were few, but my absences provoked him to find a new register. He administered his scoldings—elongated whines that rose higher and higher in pitch until they petered out in a mousey squeak—for several days after my return. When awake, he did not want me out of sight, and if I left a room while he was napping, he would rev up his whine at the instant of his awakening. At times I felt not only secure in his attachment, I felt leashed by it.

Spring provided a welcome corrective. The returning flocks of birds, the emergence of hot- and cold-blooded critters from their holes, the rising of sap and warmth, all served to whet Sebastian's appetite for independence and the hunt. For the first time in months I was able to read or write without a cat in my lap. I was even free to close the door to my study, though I learned to open it gingerly, because Sebastian had chosen its sill as the depository for his trophies. Fortunately, he showed scant interest in the birds who frequented my feeders; he specialized in rodents. I taught him by my consistent, heated reaction not to render mice unto me, but he couldn't resist showing off the occasional rarity. Always the fruit of his night-stalking, these specimens

would send me to *The Mammal Guide* first thing in the morning, where I would identify, to my amazement, a long-tailed
weasel or, alas, a flying squirrel.

For the first time since I had made him mine, Sebastian
stayed out of sight, and beyond the range of my whistles,
for two and three days at a time. I tried not to worry, and,
bolstered by his eventual returns, I succeeded. Thanks to
Rebecca, he was healthier than he had ever been, and he had
given me plentiful evidence of his survival skills. Still, I was
not prepared for a four-day disappearance in early May,
which stretched into a fifth and sixth day, and on the
seventh day became a desertion.

Countless times each day, I would climb the steep slope
of my backyard and, armed with pruning shears, enter the
woods on paths choked with spring growth, whistling and
clipping as I thrashed deeper into Sebastian's territory. I even
carried a small canteen, from which I sipped to keep my
whistle loud and clear. I flushed entire flocks of birds from
their roosts and frightened deer into blazing trails through
dense thickets; closer to home, I made the acquaintance of
several dogs who looked bewildered when they raced to
answer a summons only to be shooed away. At home, I kept
listening for the sound of a flapping rubber door; or I would
awaken to a thump in the night and come downstairs to see
if it was *the* thump.

In mid-May, when I left to visit my father, I arranged
for a house sitter who I hoped would become a cat sitter,
but when I returned home a week later, with other matters
on my mind, I knew it was time to stop whistling. I was tired
of being absorbed by absence. Spring was passing me by.

The best month of the trout season was coming to a close, and I hadn't even entered the stream, the surest source of my well-being, where I had learned to seek and find pleasure with my father's hand-me-down fly rods. I relied upon the stream for clarity, for calm; there was balance in the press of cool water against my ankles, the kiss of sun on my face. My father also relied on the stream, but this season he could only test its waters vicariously. He wanted news of the stream from me.

The morning after my return from Minnesota, I went out the front door, crossed the road, and walked through the cemetery toward the stream, my vest pockets bulging with the paraphernalia of possibility. In the shallows, my first casts were hurried, half-hearted, executed without the intense, hushed focus of expectancy. I was waiting until I reached a certain, deeper stretch of stream to fish in earnest. This deepening was my sweet spot on the stream, where I knew the location of every submerged boulder and declivity of bank, where I had caught and released so many trout that I knew them as individuals: the trout who lives beneath the overhanging boughs of hemlock, the one who jumps directly across from the abandoned beaver dam, the one who patrols the stream where it forks to the right around the island. It was the spot where I expected to see blue herons and kingfishers, sometimes muskrats or foxes or deer, where the wildflowers were most profuse, where I never encountered another human soul and where I always felt at peace.

I arrived, and all was as I remembered it, at least above the surface of the water. After taking a moment to marvel at my perversity in delaying my return to this spot, I made my first cast, to the trout I hoped was still lurking under the hemlock boughs. I felt a quick, hello tug before my line went slack: I'd lost him, but no matter, I was content to know he was still there. There was no point casting for him again, so I started wading along the bank toward the beaver dam. When the streambed changed from stones to sucking mud, I clambered up onto the bank and was startled by the sound of something large crashing through the brush. I looked toward the sound and saw a leaping flash of fur. Whatever it was, it was heading away from me, fast.

Quickly running through the inventory of possibilities—rabbit, fox, woodchuck, beaver, fawn—I concluded that none matched the size, shape, and color of what I had seen. Though distant, I could still hear the sound of its flight through the brush. I whistled. The crashing stopped. I whistled again. Silence. I let loose with my long, plaintive, single-noted "ple-e-e-ase" of a whistle. A cat cried in response, and as I continued to whistle, he leaped and cried, leaped and cried, until he could see that it was indeed me. We traded looks that asked, "What on earth are you doing here?" Then we walked the quarter mile home together, me in the stream, Sebastian close by on the bank.

Sebastian scolded me for the next several days, as if I were the one who had taken a leave of absence. For the remainder of the summer, we coordinated our departures. When he saw me packing, he got that ready-to-roam look in his eyes, and within hours of my return, I'd see his nose poking through the cat door. In September, I helped my father make the move to Pennsylvania. He reminded me of his wish to have a portion of his ashes released into the stream. I was even more certain that I knew the perfect place.

Coda

It has been five years since Sebastian took up residence on my front porch, and this winter is the coldest since the winter of his arrival. After four unseasonably mild winters that looked and felt like endless, leafless, gray falls, I had almost forgotten what a snow-covered landscape looked like. Winter arrived early and unmistakably this year with a thirty-six-inch snowfall on December 10, and frigid temperatures have kept the ground white ever since. It is late February now, and for the past several weeks, the temperature has dipped toward or below zero every night. Bright, sunny days that seldom rise above the mid-20's have baked successive snowfalls into hard-packed layers topped with a glistening crust of fresh snow. Sometimes the crust is glazed smooth, sometimes it is rippled with wind lines, like a white shore lapped by white waves. If you dig into the snow, you can read the layers like tree rings and decipher the history of the season's storms.

Sebastian has spent most of the winter curled up on the sofa, going outdoors only for brief inspection tours of the nearest reaches of his territory. He hasn't asked for much attention, and I haven't given much—to him or to anything. My brother died in October, five years to the day after our mother's death, three years to the month after our father's. I am stripped clean of family. Most of the time I just sit, immobilized by the weight of loss, a survivor like Sebastian, in whose somnolent company I take scant comfort. When the inertia begins to feel like a permanent state, I force myself to do something. I go to the store, I shovel another path in the snow, I take a trip.

Yesterday afternoon when I returned from an overnight trip to the city, Sebastian was not home. A neighbor said she had seen him earlier in the day, so I didn't concern myself with his absence until it turned dark and the temperature started its nightly dive. At nine, when the outdoor thermometer read zero, I started to worry. By midnight and -8, I was fending off morbid speculations. Over these five years I have become expert in quieting fears, but when there were no signs of Sebastian in the morning, I knew my fears were rational. Why would an animal who had chosen warmth for weeks, who had remained impervious even to the lure of full-moonlit nights, suddenly choose to endure sub-zero cold under only the slenderest of crescent moons? What if he was injured, unable to find cover? Gruesome images, graphic and unbidden, presented themselves; I tried to turn them back, but they were determined to find lodging in my mind.

At ten A.M., it was a brisk, bright 20 degrees. I dressed warmly and trudged up the snowy slope of my backyard and down the path through the woods to the glade, hoping to find tracks to follow from there. I whistled and took off my earmuffs to listen for a response. Nothing of interest. A large flock of birds scattered overhead, but I kept my gaze fixed low to the ground. The glade had been heavily trafficked since the last snow; cat prints mixed with those of dogs, rabbits, a raccoon, and various small rodents whose tracks I have not learned to distinguish. It was hard to determine how fresh any of the prints were, and which of the many cat prints might be Sebastian's most recent. To isolate his tracks from the rest, I would have to return to his starting point, the cat window, and try to find his path from there.

Ten minutes later, I was back in the glade, having arrived there this time by a route I would not have chosen for myself. Emerging from a thicket with snagged clothes and whipped cheeks, I continued to follow the selected set of paw prints as they crossed the clearing and re-entered the woods heading down toward a little creek that separates my property from the steep, high-rising, wooded hillside that places Ancram in a deeply nestled valley. The spot where the prints crossed the creek was made impassable to me by a bristling arch of head-high briars that spanned the water like a covered bridge. Moving fifty yards up-creek to a passage I had cleared in the fall, I leaped to the other side and then circled back to pick up Sebastian's tracks. On this side of the creek, there were no other sets of cat or dog prints, and since Sebastian was the widest roaming of the domestic animals in the village, I was now convinced I was on the right trail.

The prints, depressed about an inch into the top layer of snow, led steadily up and across the hillside for a hundred yards or so, and then disappeared without a trace as they approached a stand of tall pines. With each heavy plunge of my boots through thin crust into deep snow, I had braced for the sight of a cat stopped dead in his tracks, but I was not prepared for a vanishing, as if Sebastian had been beamed up to a better place. Or perhaps I was seeing signs of his metamorphosis, not into a winged but a hoofed creature. A clear set of deer prints picked up where Sebastian's left off. For lack of any other clue, I began following this new set of prints, which in due course split in two; the deer had headed farther uphill, and from out of his prints emerged a cat's heading downhill. For a moment, I thought stealth was Sebastian's motive for hiding his prints in the deer's larger, deeper, harder-packed tracks, but then I realized he was probably making use of a ready-made path to spare his frozen footpads the stinging effort of breaking through the snow's clinging crust.

Now that his prints were on a downhill course through the woods, I was pretty sure I knew his destination, which I could reach by a more direct route, but I kept following his trail to make sure nothing had befallen him on the way. His prints led, as I suspected they would, all the way down the hill, then skirted the southern side of the old one-room schoolhouse that is Ancram's town hall, and crossed County Route 7 at a point about a quarter mile distant from my house, but almost twice that far by Sebastian's overhill route. From there, he headed down a dirt road through private property that abuts my sweet spot on the stream. As I approached the end of the dirt road, I whistled and Sebastian immediately showed himself. Standing on a fallen log, crying and looking pitiful as he kneaded the snow with his front paws, he seemed to reproach me for taking so long to reclaim him. But when I tried to lead him back down the road toward home, he wouldn't follow.

After a long duet of whistles and cries, I was finally made to understand that he didn't want to follow me home along the road, and he didn't want to return by the route he had come; he preferred to complete the circle round his territory by taking a path that ran along the stream toward home. I obliged him by blazing a trail of deep, dragging boot prints in which Sebastian happily followed through a field of drifted snow into the narrow strip of woods that separated us from the stream.

When we reached the ridge above the stream, the sun was high enough in a clear blue sky for its warmth to reach us through the bare branches of trees from which a large flock of birds flitted and called. As if startled awake from a deep sleep, I suddenly realized what I was seeing. The birds were robins, as were the flock I had stirred into flight above the glade when I was too lost in worry to notice. And the thick cross-hatching of prints in the glade, didn't they include creatures who should still be in their burrows? It had been so long since I mixed my prints with theirs that I'd lost track of where we were in the cycle. The blackness inside and the whiteness outside had blinded me to the signs of another spring. It wasn't there yet, but it was on its way.

As we walked along the ridge, the stream sparkled up at me for the first time since October. When we approached a ravine cut into the ridge by a rivulet that flows into the stream, Sebastian stopped for a minute to sharpen his claws on a tree trunk. He then raced ahead of me, sprinted down the ravine, bounded from rock to rock across the water, dashed up the other side, and without a pause leaped onto the vertical trunk of a tree that he scaled for twenty feet before reaching a suitable branch on which to strike a proud leonine pose. I whistled my admiration, and then I improvised another tune for my thanks.

It seems we are wed to this repetition, each the other's link to this cycle of loss and recovery. In these years, I have come to rely upon his capacity for survival, his power to transform my fear of ending into an anticipation of spring.

FROM ASHES

⌒ IT WAS THE FIRST spring after my father's death, and he was often on my mind. After a mild, tedious, gray, and lingering winter, the garden and the stream beckoned at last, asking for and easily drawing my attention as they had every spring since I'd moved to the country. Five springs out of Manhattan, I was still a relative newcomer to nature, so questions followed closely in the wake of my attention. In April, when the forsythias and daffodils bloomed, I wondered if there was a reason yellow things flowered first. When the dahlia bulbs, still stored in brown paper bags for their overwinter rest in the basement, began sending up pale shoots a month earlier than usual, I wanted to let them turn green in earth and air. But if I planted bulbs a month early, would they bloom a month early, when the intense sun of early August would bleach the scarlet vibrancy from their velvety petals?

In the stream, I wondered what kind of fly would lure trout in water that was seasonably high but unseasonably warm, swollen by rains rather than melted snow. Several times a week I would head impulsively for the phone with my questions and be caught up short with the realization that no one was waiting on the other end of the line with answers.

Since moving to the country, spring had become the season of our surest connection, when we were linked by pleasures that were new to me, long sustaining to my father. In the garden and the stream, he was my teacher, my guide; and with this changed venue of authority, for the first time since childhood, I did not grow bristly with impatience at the disciplines he counseled.

In settings more like his, I was becoming more like my father. It was not a conscious process, although I was made aware of it by a friend's casual remark. She said that she liked watching me use my hands, that there was something unusual about it she couldn't quite define. The observation didn't engage my attention until some months later, when the same friend met my father for the first time and was struck by a similarity in our hands. Not a similarity of appearance, she said, but of use, which she described this time as seeming "studied."

I started to watch. I noticed the way my father tied the flies I use to fish for trout. I noticed the way he gathered seeds from his flowers, the way he opened a jar or closed a window, the way he washed a dish or applied a coat of paint.

I noticed the way he stroked my mother's cheek with the back of his cupped fingers to soothe her pain. The way he removed a bandage, zipped up a jacket, or brushed snow from a windshield.

His hands never hurried or forced their will on anything, not even on the stubborn, stuck lid of a jar. He seemed to use his hands to understand the nature of whatever he touched, to discover how things worked and what they wanted. They were intelligent hands, careful, gentle, and infinitely patient. I should have known. Patience was everywhere in him. In the even tones of his voice, in the unvaried steadiness of his stride, in his almost reflexive "We'll see" response to requests for immediate action. Patience was the virtue I both admired and resisted in him, keenly feeling its double edge, so reassuring when lavished upon one, so maddening when urged.

Some of that patience must have seeped into my hands, especially when tending to things that depended upon my care: flowers and cats and home, my mother's and then my father's flesh. My hands had become more like his, and yet they looked very different. Mine were nicked and scratched. My patience, unlike his, had bounds. My hands, unlike his, bore the marks of fitful impulsivity. Pinched by the window sash that stuck and then yielded to excessive pressure all at once. Clawed by the stray who was less curious than I was. Torn by the thorns that stood between me and ripe raspberries or by the brambled branch that offered the only handhold when a muddy bank gave way.

A childhood of scraped knees was being recapitulated in middle age on the backs of my hands. My father, who taught by example rather than reproof, suggested I always carry a tube of Neosporin in my pocket. I gladly took his advice, knowing its impetus was antibacterial, not anti-impulse. In our last five years, with similarities in fuller view, it had become easier for both of us to acknowledge the value, as well as the intransigence, of our differences. In the last year of his life, the mutual acknowledgments became increasingly open, no longer coded in the language of ointment.

The October my father died, I knew I was fortunate to feel we had left little of importance unsaid. The following spring, though still spared that keenest of regrets, I discovered another. There may have been little more to say, but there was so much more to learn, now lost to me with him. There would be no more borrowing from his experience. The trial and error would be my own, not by choice, as it had so often been, but of necessity.

Not long after I registered this finality, I discovered I had one more lesson to learn from my father, through what remained of him on earth. When he had asked me to cast a portion of his ashes into the trout stream that wends through Ancram, I had said I would release them at the riffles, where the buck crossed, where the blue heron fished, where I had caught my first brown trout on a fly he tied. He had smiled and so had I, taking early consolation for anticipated loss. After his death, I waited for spring, for days of long light and warm air, to fulfill my promise.

Now spring had arrived, and another lesson was waiting for me with his ashes, stored out of sight for the winter in a small brass container placed on the bottom shelf of a closed bookcase in an unused guest bedroom. I was about to learn that the consolations of nature, though real, are never so easily attained in reality as they are in the imagination.

Weather was my first foil. The spring that arrived that year in upstate New York bore little resemblance to the spring my imagination had forecast. There was, for instance, little light. There was instead a lot of rain. After a winter of historically low snowfall came a spring so wet that drought warnings gave way to flood alerts within a matter of days. Streams that had dwindled to a trickle over the winter suddenly rose and surged over their banks, making the opening weeks of trout season fit only for the very tall and foolhardy. Hip boots offer no protection in water that is chin high.

Throughout April and May, day after rainy day, the Roecliff Jansen Kill continued to rise. During breaks in the weather, I would go, fly rod in hand, to the stretch of stream pictured in those photographs I had sent to my father. Standing on the flooded bank in knee-deep water, I watched rampaging currents carry uprooted trees toward the next bend in the stream where they were added to a stockpile of broken limbs. Even the shallow riffles had become white-water rapids. One step off the bank, and I would have been swept along with my father's ashes to the same final resting place.

But high water was not all that kept me from entering the stream. This stretch of the Roe Jan had been despoiled. Not visually. Although turbulence had changed the contours of the stream, broadened and deepened its bed, cut into its banks and felled trees, turbulence had not destroyed the stream's beauty; rioting waters had simply turned its pastoral beauty wild. The violation wasn't visual; it was olfactory. A foul odor permeated the air.

The source of the odor was no mystery. I could see it, even touch it, if I wanted to. It was emanating from a growing mound of pinkish-brown sludge that was being dumped in a clearing about eighty yards from the bank where I stood. I thought of this stretch of stream as mine because in the three years since I first came upon it, I had never seen anyone else there. Maybe it was just that nobody else chose to ignore the NO TRESPASSING signs posted by the small paper mill that owned the property affording the only easy access to its bank.

For three years, by car or on foot, I had passed through an open chain-link gate on mill property and followed a rutted dirt road to its end. From there I sloshed through eighty yards of marsh to arrive at my fishing hole. There were other ways of arriving at the spot from the opposite bank, on land not owned by the mill, but they involved much more trekking, through several hundred yards of prickly brush and then over the slippery stones of the streambed for another several hundred yards until you arrived at the riffles. So the mill route was by far the most convenient, and I had come to take it for granted.

Of course, this route had its drawbacks. Although the mill road was suitably pastoral, flanked by a marsh that was home to large flocks of red-winged blackbirds and several dozen species of wildflowers, it came to its end at a clearing that was home to a clutch of parked bulldozers. When I first came upon it, the clearing was flat, scraped bare earth, and the dozers sat idle. The second summer, the dozers were mobilized to create a hill. The men operating them never objected to my trespassing or questions, so I learned that the

mill had been ordered by the state to close and cover a landfill at the spot. When I later asked a mill executive, who was
also the town supervisor, what had been dumped there, so
near the stream, he assured me it was "harmless stuff, cardboard boxes and the like."

Not knowing how to pursue the matter further, I chose
to believe him, and so as I picked my way through the deep,
muddy ruts of the mill road on the opening day of trout season the following spring, I hoped to see a grassy hillock
where a mound of trash had been. Instead I was met by the
stench rising from the pile of pink sludge that was growing
next to a grassy hillock. One hand for my rod, one for my
nose, I sloshed through the sucking mud of the marsh to the
stream, which rose over its bank to meet me.

Despite an anger, both visceral and righteous, at this
defilement, I was reluctant to assert my trespasser's right to a
fresh-smelling fishing hole. I knew the mill and its environ-
mental practices were sensitive subjects in my small town.
Although Ancram (pop. 1,533) covers nearly a hundred
square miles of rolling farmland, its village center, which
houses most of the nonfarming population, including me, is
just a few dozen houses scattered around a bend in the Roe
Jan, where a natural thirty-foot waterfall lured industry to
town as early as 1743. During the Revolutionary War, iron
forged at Ancram became cannonballs and the enormous
links of a chain strung across the Hudson to prevent the
British from sailing upriver. A mill of one sort or another has
operated at the same site for as long as there has been a village, and most residents feel that if Ancram is to exist for
another 250 years, there had always better be one.

If a villager doesn't work at the mill, he is likely to have a brother, uncle, cousin, wife, or daughter-in-law who does. We all have a routinely re-elected town supervisor who does. So if the black smoke that belches from the mill on bad days coats your laundry with soot, you just wash it again. And if you find yourself downwind of a bad smell, you just get yourself upwind.

I had learned how the town felt about the mill during the laundry crisis of 1988. It had been a particularly hot, dry summer, when people's wells were low and tempers were high. The families living on Poole Hill Road, just downwind of the smokestacks, were getting tired of running out of water after rewashing clothes that had grown black while they were hung out to dry. But many of the people living on Poole Hill Road had jobs at the mill, and when they brought their complaints to work, they were told to choose between their laundry and their living. After the Ancram Day Festival in mid-July, when the whole village had gathered on the dusty ball-fields of the town park to run three-legged races and watch the smoke billowing from the mill's stacks gather into a huge, black cloud that hung low over our heads for hours, a few people were ready to protest.

As a newcomer, with none of my strings attached to the mill, I was asked to sound the alarm. After a couple weeks of telephone shuttling between various state and county agencies, I managed to learn enough about the regulations governing the expulsion of black and white smoke to know that the mill was violating them. And I had pried loose the name of the state official responsible for making the mill clean up its stacks. But before I could get him to return my calls, I was summoned to my father's sickbed in Minnesota. The day before I left Ancram, I gave my list of names and numbers to one of the villagers who had enlisted my help.

I was out of Ancram, in body and mind, until late October, when I returned home after my father's funeral. When I asked what had become of our efforts to whiten the mill's smoke, the woman who had taken over for me said that her daughter, who works at the mill, asked her to please drop the issue. The mill supervisors had made it known that if Ancram didn't like black smoke, the company could always find another town that did.

So the next spring, when I came across the growing mound of smelly sludge, I didn't know how to proceed. Should I rise to the defense of my fishing hole at the possible expense of my neighbors' livelihood? It was possible, of course, that much more than the aesthetics of my fishing hole was at stake. Since the sludge was being dumped within a few yards of marshland that sent rivulets straight into the stream during rainy seasons like this one, there was no doubt that whatever chemicals the sludge contained would leach into the stream and course through farmland, to be lapped up by deer and beavers and dairy cows. Most of the kids in town fished from a readily accessible stretch of bank less than a quarter mile downstream from my fishing hole, and most of their parents were happy to live on a spring diet of brown trout.

Some days I convinced myself that the food chain of the entire county was being jeopardized. Other days I suspected myself of concocting a speculative threat to the larger good to rationalize my own selfish interest in the purity of my favorite stretch of stream. Every day I felt the weight of my unfulfilled promise to my father, whose ashes still rested in their shiny brass container on the bottom shelf of the bookcase. Still, I did not act. The high waters of April and May provided me with an excuse for making my father wait, and in June I left for a trip to Italy, to the hilltop in Tuscany where my father and mother and I had spent our happiest times together as adults, where my father and I had returned two summers earlier after my mother's death, and where I now returned alone.

When I came home in early July, I found the stream lower, the pile of sludge higher. If I didn't act soon, the days of long light would grow short without my ever having entered the stream. I berated myself daily for my inertia. Why was I so reluctant to act? Was I cowed by the mill's power, afraid of reprisal or shunning? After so recent a loss of both parents, was I afraid of disturbing the shallow roots that made this town my home? Or was it possible I didn't want to carry out the promise I made to my father? Perhaps I was afraid to risk discovering that no ritual could bear the power of consolation I had endowed it with in my imagination. Maybe I just wasn't ready to say good-bye, and the smelly pile of pink sludge allowed a delay that I wanted.

What finally spurred me to action was not the resolution of any of these questions, but the arrival of Alice. Alice, who had cared for my father during the last, difficult year of his life, came from Minnesota to visit me for a week in mid-July. She knew of my promise and hoped to join me in its fulfillment. Although I bore Alice a great debt of gratitude for the kindness she had lavished on my widowed and dying father, I did not want to share this last farewell to him with anyone. There had been other, more public memorials, where Newton B. Schreiber had been mourned as friend, colleague, brother, uncle, grandfather, where my own very particular loss had been subsumed and nearly lost in a general grief. When I entered the stream with his ashes, I wanted solitude, privacy to honor the bond that existed only between my father and me.

Torn between gratitude and possessiveness, I tested the mix of my emotions one day by driving Alice down the mill road to its end. As soon as Alice opened the car door, she winced at the smell and, quickly slamming the door shut, suggested we find another spot on the stream for the ashes—right away. Her words unlocked my adrenaline. Suddenly, my course was clear. I couldn't put my father's ashes in a befouled stretch of stream, and no place but the promised one would do. I must clean up the stream. I would take courage from my father and do battle. Alice immediately saw the fitness of this course of action, even though it meant the ashes would stay in the bookshelf during her visit.

That afternoon, I called the county health department to talk to a man who had been sympathetic about the black smoke. After I explained my mission, he gave me the number of the state office in charge of solid waste disposal. I called and received unconvincing assurances that someone would get back to me shortly. Several days passed without the promised call, but in the meantime, I found an ally.

As I was leaving The Little Store one morning after my daily chat with the owner, I was stopped by her sister, Dottie, who lives downwind from the mill. Dottie said she couldn't stand the disgusting odor that wafted from mill property toward her kitchen door—would I sign a petition? We struck a partnership on the spot. She would seek signatures from townspeople while I sought action from government officials. She didn't expect to get much satisfaction from the mill and warned me not to expect much from the state.

A week later, I received a call from a state official who apologized for his delay in reaching me. Even more astonishingly, he admitted he was the very man who had given the mill permission to dump the sludge from its pollution filtration system on mill property after the county landfill was closed last fall. He insisted the sludge was "innocuous, suitable for land cover," but since it was causing an odor, and since it was closer to wetlands and stream than he realized, the sludge would have to go. He promised to write the mill a letter ordering them to stop dumping the sludge immediately and to remove whatever had already been stockpiled. "That's all there is to it?" I asked. "No," he said. "They'll probably get very upset and insist there is no other way for them to dispose of their waste."

When I called him a week later to find out how the mill had responded, he said he hadn't heard a thing, which surprised him, because he had expected vehement objections. The next morning I learned that Dottie had received a response to her petition, which she had wisely sent to the national headquarters of The Kimberly-Clark Corporation, the most recent owner of Ancram's small mill. In a politely worded letter, the president of the specialty products division said that the mill wanted to be "a good neighbor," and so he had arranged for off-site disposal of any new sludge.

The old sludge would be covered immediately to eliminate the odor and then removed in the fall. There was no mention of having been ordered to do so by state authorities.

Later that week, I walked to the mill road to see if they were keeping their promise. What I found, for the first time in three years, was a padlocked gate barring my entrance to the road. For a minute I entertained the thought that they had locked the gate to hide evidence of their noncompliance, but then I noticed traces of pink sludge, embossed with wavy tire-tread marks, on the paved road leading away from the mill. Clearly, they were keeping their word, and since they had closed the dump site, there was no need to leave the gate open for sludge-bearing trucks. Or perhaps they were just tired of trespassers. Whatever their motive, I had just lost access to my fishing hole.

I spent the next several weeks trying to find an alternate route, my urgency fueled by the knowledge that trout season was already well past its prime. First, I looked for a way to get down the steep bank behind the Lutheran Cemetery, which sits on a rise just across the road from my house. The twenty-foot slope to the stream was nearly vertical and choked with brambles except for one patch where a pile of broken tree branches had been tossed over the edge. Using the branches as a ladder, I clambered down to level ground at some risk to fly rod and limbs, then struggled through ten yards of ankle-deep mud to the stream and began inching my way downstream toward the fishing hole.

Hard experience had taught me to move slowly over the streambed; it had also taught me to cover every inch of exposed skin and hair with Deep Woods Off, which repels

every insect it says it does except for biting deerflies, which
were out in force. They swarmed so densely around my head
while I was trying to negotiate one fast-flowing stretch of
water that I whacked fistfuls of them every few seconds as I
stumbled downstream with eyes shut tight and both arms
flailing. Finally I arrived at the deeper, slower waters of my
fishing hole, and the flies miraculously disappeared. As if
rewarding me for grace under pressure, the stream offered
me three good-sized trout, bing, bing, bing.

After so long a layoff from fishing, my release technique was a little rusty, so each time I got a fish on the line,
I maneuvered it toward a fallen log near the bank, where I
could sit down and gently work out the hook. I was easing a
fourth fish toward the log when I heard a loud, scuttling
noise behind me. I turned around, lost the fish and saw a wet
beaver snout sticking out of the brush on the bank directly
behind the fallen log. Enjoying the novelty of a beaver at my
fishing hole, I tried to talk him out of hiding. After a few
minutes of my cajoling, he emerged from the brush to show
his whole body and started talking back, with the kind of
low moan Sebastian uses to greet strange animals who have
invaded his territory.

A few minutes later he entered the water and headed
straight for me. Heedless of the slippery stones beneath
me, I ran full speed across the stream and leapt up to what
I hoped was the safety of the other bank. From there I
watched him swim in circles around the fishing hole, moan-
ing all the while. I now realized that when I perched on the
fallen log to release the trout, I was sitting on this beaver's
new home. I had heard no local lore about attack beavers,

but there was no doubt in my mind that this beaver was provoked. When he (or she) finally swam downstream and
vanished into my side of the bank, it occurred to me that he
might try to sneak through the brush and ambush me.
Thinking more clearly, I decided the skirmish was over and
it was time for me to retreat. Next time, I would establish
more cordial relations by not sitting on his home.

A few days later the cemetery route was impassable.
More fallen branches had been added to the pile in crisscross
fashion, making it an open invitation to break a leg. The only
alternative was to trespass on the wooded land adjacent to the
cemetery and crash through two hundred yards of dense
brush to the stream. Propelled by sheer willfulness, I arrived
at my destination in shreds, thrashed my way downstream
through a black fog of bloodthirsty deerflies, and greeted the
beaver who awaited me with a low moan of my own. He dove
under and stayed out of sight, as did the trout.

After a couple hours of fruitless casting, I was ready to
call it a day but loath to face the gauntlet of flies and briars
again. Why not look for a downstream exit? I thought. I knew
there was a bridge not more than a quarter mile down the
road, which runs roughly parallel to the stream, and although
I had never explored this particular stretch of the Roe Jan,
how treacherous could it be in mid-August when the stream
was at its lowest? It was nearing the end of a beautiful afternoon, with sunlight slanting almost sideways through the tree
trunks, burnishing woods and stream gold, a good time to
pull in my line and enjoy an early-evening wade.

I started in water that was only ankle deep as it forked
around the slender island that marks the downstream bound-

ary of the fishing hole. A flock of cedar waxwings, satiny olive green with black bandit eye masks, crisscrossed the stream, staying just a few yards ahead of me, snatching and scattering the insects before they could ambush me. When I passed the island and entered a deeper stretch where the two forks rejoin, I saw a great blue heron lift off and disappear over the treetops in four strong flaps of his enormous wings. As I continued downstream, the water deepened, but when it lapped my waist, I simply moved closer to one of the banks and it receded to knee level.

I had been wading for a half hour when the streambed suddenly changed from rock to mud. I tried moving toward midstream, but the water rose past my waist to my chest, so I decided to stay near the bank even though it meant nearly losing my sneakers to suction with each hard-won footstep. Another fifteen minutes of hugging the bank and I was in water up to my shoulders with no obvious way to proceed. A fallen tree, its branches intact, blocked my passage along the bank. The opposite bank was clear of debris, but to reach it I would have to swim across the stream in water that was probably over my head. The other choice was to backtrack through the mud to shallower water upstream and then cross to the other bank. Since it was getting dark and I didn't know how far I would have to backtrack or what I would find midstream on those untested waters either, I decided to swim.

The stream was only fifteen or twenty yards wide at this point, and though the water was deep, the current looked slow. Slow enough for the one-armed paddle-wheel stroke I would have to do, fully clothed and holding my eight-foot fly rod aloft with my free hand. I took one step farther from the bank and lost all choice in the matter. I was in water over my head, inhaling a current that was stronger than it had looked an instant before, especially since it had sneakers, jeans, a long-sleeved shirt thick enough to serve as bug armor, and a fishing vest with a half-dozen bulging pockets to tug against. There was no way I could get fifteen yards cross stream without being carried a hundred yards downstream toward who knew what; propelled by panic, I strenuously thrashed my way to the bank I had just left and reconciled myself to the long slog upstream, back to the fishing hole and on through the biting flies to the brush.

After that episode I was determined to find a safe, reliable route to the fishing hole. Walking back and forth along County Route 7 in search of likely entries from the road, I noticed a faint tractor path at the edge of a hayfield that led from the road toward the stream. But before I explored it, I decided to find out who owned the field. I wanted explicit permission to use this route, not because of any newfound scruples about trespassing, but because I didn't want to find myself suddenly barred from the premises by an irritated owner who does not share my feeling about the inalienable right to stream access. Besides, I would probably need to hack a path through the strip of woods that separated the hayfield from the stream, so there was little likelihood my presence would go unnoticed.

I explained my purpose to Betty, the owner of The Little Store, and asked if she knew who owned the property across from Town Hall. She said she wasn't sure who owned the field, but the property right next to it was hers, and I was welcome to use it. She told me to follow a long dirt driveway that led to a house hidden from the road; years ago, she said, before her mother died, there had been a path that led straight from the house to a little island where they used to picnic. I told her that was the exact spot I was trying to reach, and she said I could open up a new path anytime I wanted. "Mother would love it," she said, clearly pleased that this section of stream meant as much to me as it once had to her.

On Labor Day, a friend and I, armed with pruning clippers and a scythe, walked down that dirt driveway. We beat a short path through a narrow strip of meadow and then carved a wide boulevard through the 150 feet of woods that stood between the meadow and the stream. There would be no stumbling on this path, no low overhead branches to snag my fly rod or force me into a crouch. I could walk tall down this path to my fishing hole as if I were making a stately processional down the main aisle of a church to the altar. There would be no pratfalls with my father's ashes.

Since the days of long light had passed, I thought I might as well wait until October 2, the first anniversary of my father's death. But two days later, about noon on a clear, sunny September 6, I was overtaken by a sudden, unshakable feeling that the moment had come. The light was less intense than it would have been earlier in the summer, but the air was as soft and beckoning as any day on earth.

I went straight to the bookcase. Five minutes later, I had parked my car in the dirt driveway and was heading toward the path carrying a freshly polished brass container inscribed NBS, 1914–1988. With my first step into the meadow, I flushed a brace of mourning doves whose whistling wing beats first startled and then elated me. I walked slowly, surrounded by the loud buzzing of bees in head-high goldenrod. When I entered the wooded part of the path, I stepped carefully over the moss-covered trunk of a fallen tree. Finally I reached the stream. The water that kept me stranded on the bank in May was now only ankle deep at the edges, barely knee deep midstream.

I waded upstream toward the riffles, staying near the bank rather than risking a stumble in deeper water. Hearing a throaty rattle overhead, I looked up and spied a kingfisher, perched heavy-headed on a treetop high above the water. I paused to take in the beauty of this day, this place, the far bank splashed with drifting waves of wildflowers—tall stands of purple loosestrife and goldenrod, the tufted pink tops of Joe Pye weed nodding over creamy disks of Queen Anne's lace. Nearer me, on the more shaded bank, a low cluster of blue forget-me-nots nestled under two brilliant red spires of cardinal flower. As I stood still, letting my eyes roam, something in the profusion made me aware of the ring I was wearing, a ring that had been my mother's. I remembered the day she found it, desired it, not because its stone was precious, which it wasn't, but because something about it seemed to contain the pleasure of that afternoon in Florence. My mind blinked at the memory, confounded by the image of three together, rapt by Italy and innocent of the designs upon them. Only four summers ago. How impossible it would have been to conceive this day then.

The disjunction was too great. I shook my head, bringing my focus back to the stream, my mission, and looked ahead of me to the riffles. After resurrecting the buck's crossing in my mind's eye, I waded upstream to the exact spot of his exit and then turned to face the other bank. Midstream, I sat on a large boulder, the riffles rushing round my feet as I prepared myself for this release, so long anticipated, so long delayed. I held the brass container in my hand, studied its inscription, and saw not only the lettering but also the clear reflection of blue sky, white clouds, green trees, and my own face in its polished surface. I laughed out loud at the sight of myself in this odd mirror, my father's initials etched upon my lips, his dates across my chin.

I stood up and moved a few steps downstream until I felt sunlight full on my face. Then I pried off the lid, removed the plastic bag from the container, and looked closely at the ashes for the first time since they had entered my possession. As clearly as I had seen my face mirrored in brass, I saw in the ashes not only my father's fate but also my own. I shuddered at this stark vision and felt a strong reluctance to reach inside the bag and take the ashes in my hand. Then I remembered it would be my last touch of my father's flesh. I recalled the intimacy we had learned to share when he finally let me dress his wounds, and I did not want to shrink from this last hard task. I reached in, felt the coarse grain of this powder against my palm and fed a fistful to the stream. I did this four times and then bent down to rinse the last particles of my father from my hand. Standing up, I looked at the water coursing downstream and felt something well up in me. I felt a deep sadness that brought tears to my eyes, which added their slight flow to the stream that was carrying my father's ashes to places perhaps more distant than I can imagine. But I also felt a powerful wave of relief rising and cresting within me. I had fulfilled my promise, and my reward was a sudden explosion within me of all the love that was contained in its making.

A life flashed before me—not his or mine, but the separate life that existed between us. I felt the love he bore me as an infant, that I returned to him as an adoring child, the fierce protective passion that blazed from him when he would carry me home bleeding from childhood injuries, that blazed from me when I stood guard over him as he lay paralyzed from the waist down in his hospital bed that last day. I remembered the extremity of those final hours, when in a rare, unexpected twist of his rare disease, he lost his adult mind but not his adult strength, when he broke the hold of two orderlies trying to restrain him and grabbed my head in a stranglehold, bending it down toward him. Before the orderlies, who feared for my neck in the tight vise of his right arm, could intervene, he kissed the top of my head and said, "This is my daughter." Then he released me. It was the mark of my father that I never suspected the full extent of his strength until those last hours when he no longer had the power to check it.

I took a deep breath and walked downstream to my newly carved path, certain that our connection exists as surely now as it did in any of those moments. Approaching home, looking toward my garden, I saw the dahlias blooming brilliantly in the gentle September sun. In the spring, listening to a voice that counseled patience, I had made the right decision. The scarlet dahlias, progeny of bulbs my father had harvested from his mother's garden and nourished for decades in his own, had not faded. Neither had the voice that guided me in their care. I could hear it anytime—in the garden, in the stream.

PART 2

WAVES

HOME

⌒ 1010 MAIN STREET, Evanston, Illinois. It was the platonic ideal of a Midwestern address. The very sound of it thumped and ticked with the beat of the heartland. I pronounced it proudly for my kindergarten readiness test, right after showing evidence of my shoe-tying skills and just before drawing a blank on the what's-your-phone-number question. I loved the mnemonic tom-tom beat of that perfect address, so much easier to commit to memory than the nonsense clauses of the Nicene Creed, which was our first task of learning, before ABCs or coloring inside the lines, at St. Nicholas Grammar School.

"*Credo in unum Deum,*" we chanted in incomprehension, sitting still (no squirming) on the "magic carpet" at Sister

Alexine's feet, *"Patrem omnipotentem."* After mornings on the carpet, 1010 Main Street had the ring of release. But, sad to say, it rang as false as the words "going to school," whose jingling syllables had stirred a thrill of anticipation in me for as long as I could remember. In reality, the studio apartment in which I spent my first six years was as constricting as that scratchy, short-piled muck-gray magic carpet. More cage than home, its ochre walls contained the makings of the ideal suburban foursome of the 1950s—mother, father, big brother, little sister. But first we had to wait for the 1950s, and the building of the suburbs.

I had been born in early August, 1945, two days before the Enola Gay made history. My first experience of the larger world came when air raid sirens crowing the sudden dawn of the Atomic Age caused a panicked evacuation of St. Francis Hospital's nursery. As a hand-me-down crib was being readied for my arrival at 1010 Main, a dropped bomb named "Little Boy" had made the boom heard by housing contractors 'round the world. The first world, that is, the world that would soon be welcoming its soldiers home from war.

The problem was that for many returning veterans, though the welcome was real and joyous, "home" had become a metaphor. During sixteen years of depression and war, the loud buzz and bang of housing construction had subsided to a faint hum. Housing was in such short supply at war's end that 250 trolley cars were sold as homes in Chicago. Surplus grain bins were recycled as apartments in North Dakota, and in Omaha, a newspaper advertised a "Big Ice Box, 7 x 17, could be fixed up to live in." As families reunited, formed, and expanded throughout the late 1940s, they created a demand for housing unprecedented in history.

Like most families, we bided our time while the war machine changed gears. The apartment was our holding bin. Every night for six years, I was stored away in that hand-me-down crib, its barred sides only inches from the windowless walls of the dressing closet that served as my bedroom. I woke each dim day to the sight of my father's trousers hanging overhead. The closet also served as the only passageway between the living room, where my parents slept in a Murphy bed, and the bathroom, whose door was left ajar so I could see the light left on to keep me company.

Each morning I watched the traffic to and from the bathroom through the slats of my crib, as father got ready for work and brother for school. When they were gone, I was allowed out of the closet to play in the space made available by the raising of the Murphy bed. I never knew where my brother, Michael, slept during those years, but he later told me he spent nights in the galley kitchen, on a folding cot that was stored out of sight during the hours I was free to roam. I don't know what happened to that cot, but I thought it grimly fitting when I used those crib slats to make a guillotine for a high-school project on *A Tale of Two Cities*.

For several of those early years, I saw more of Mrs. Reese, our realtor, than of my father, who worked long hours in downtown Chicago making the money to buy the house Mrs. Reese might find us one day. On weekdays, Mrs. Reese, who resides in my memory primarily as a rancid smell of uncertain source, would drive my mother and me from house to house, all of which were too old and dark for my mother's liking, or too costly for my father's budget. On weekends, my brother and I stood in the narrow space behind the two seats of my father's Studebaker, listening spellbound to the creaking doors and spooky laughs of *The Shadow*, as we made the same futile rounds *en famille*.

I have no memory whatsoever of the many houses I must have seen, but I do remember the afternoon when my brother, who had been left in the car to watch me, decided to see what would happen if he stuck my right index finger into the dashboard cigarette lighter. My heat-seeking scream brought my father rocketing out the front door of some dark, old house, bounding down steps and running as I had never seen him before. It's not the feel or smell of singed flesh that I remember, but the awesome sight and sound of my father enraged, a spectacle I had never before witnessed, nor would I ever again. And Mike, though he still hated me for ruining his four-year idyll as an only child, was a good boy, a favorite of the nuns and priests, as I would be, too; Mike, whom my parents had cast in the lifelong role of my protector, never did another memorably mean thing to me for the rest of his days.

Each Sunday evening for five years, our hopes postponed for another week, we four trekked up the three flights of stairs to our living/sleeping/dining/playing/reading room. My memories of that apartment are vague, memories less of event than of a climate defined by a disturbing, unnatural light—gray by day and yellow by night. Not a silvery or golden glow, but the drab of dirty dishwater and old newspapers. There was bright, clean light in the little park across the street, where I ran and jumped and climbed my heart out every day of every season, but it never found a way inside.

I don't know why that apartment repelled light. I'm sure there was at least one window facing the park, because I remember that when I was old enough to play in the park by myself but not old enough to cross busy Main Street, I would holler for my mother from the curb when I wanted to come home. After two or three lung-bursting bellows, I would see her stick her head out a third-floor window, and, her beautiful face framed by red brick, she would cast her all-seeing eyes on the traffic below, signaling me with a wave when it was safe to cross.

I never once disobeyed the wait-and-holler rule, in part because I relished the rare opportunity to yell. Once inside the apartment, the gray and yellow light, so different from the white and blue of the park, seemed to contain a hush; the very air of the apartment affected me like a finger held against the lips of an expressionless face. I now think some of that grayness, which seeped around my mother and me when we were alone during the day, must have been sadness. Both my grandfathers and my mother's youngest brother had died in the eighteen months before I was born. Every family had its losses then, which is perhaps why little was ever said of those deaths, then or later. These three were mourned silently, in a gray light I would recognize forty years later, after my own three losses.

But if I was an unknowing witness to mourning, that was not the only source of the silence that reigned in our apartment. The hush I understood was a deliberate muffling, a tamping down, which I don't remember as oppressive, not exactly. I understood that it was the silence and restraint of consideration, for my father trying to read the newspaper in the yellow light, for my big brother doing his important homework, for the policeman in the apartment below who worked at night and slept in the gray light of day, for my mother, who would get in trouble if any of them, especially the policeman, were disturbed by me. I imagined Big John Weber asleep downstairs in his blue uniform, his billy club and gun at the ready. I had no concept of off duty. Being a policeman was not a job, like my father had a job, but a twenty-four-hour state of being, like my father was a father. Or like priests and nuns, cowboys and Indians, who *were* what they wore.

We were governed by the silence of small quarters, and its hold on me lasted long after the space around us expanded. To this day I am unnerved by loudness. I feel an instinctive recoil, as if I expect raised volume to bring on the angry banging of a cosmic billy club against heating pipes. To me, all loudness is alike, but silence is infinitely various. I can calibrate precisely its capacity for constricting or expanding the soul.

When we moved in 1951, we brought along the silence, which had come to feel like peace, but we left the darkness behind. Our first house was on a small lot in the newly developing part of our old Chicago suburb. The eastern edge of Evanston was, and still is, remarkable for the stately mansions that line the shore of Lake Michigan. From its opulent east, the town ascended on a slight but steady upgrade west, away from the lake toward Ridge Boulevard, a grand elm-shaded avenue of churches and other monuments to civic virtue. Continuing west from Ridge, Evanston began a gradual descent down the other side of the glacial moraine that underlay its history, past several blocks of modest brick homes to the flatlands that now beckoned to contractors. Emboldened by federal mortgage guarantees and what was now a full two decades of pent-up demand, builders began construction of a record-breaking 1,692,000 American houses in 1950, and our new home was one of the first to reach completion.

Evanston's far west was a prairie frontier when we moved in—just a grid of streets superimposed on flat fields of tall grasses and weeds. What became our neighborhood must have been zoned in the 1920s or early 30s, its streets named and paved, its small lots defined, before the Depression stopped Evanston's westward expansion in its tracks. Like the older sections of town, it had front side-walks for strolling and back alleys for sneaking. Fathers drove the family car at a snail's pace down straight, narrow streets, which intersected at proper right angles and were named for American presidents. They parked for the night in detached, one-car garages that had not yet been given pride of place; garages and garbage cans faced the alley. Second cars were unimaginable, as were the wider curving "lanes" and "drives" and "terraces" of later suburban developments, which took their names from the meadows and prairies and ridges they supplanted.

The street grid was traditional, but our house was not. To my great pleasure, Mrs. Reese's place in our life had been usurped by Mr. Dowd, our architect, a man of inexpressible glamour. He looked so much like the movie star

Jeff Chandler that, as I told my first-grade classmates at St. Nicholas, I was almost certain he *was* Jeff Chandler, perhaps rendered amnesiac by a war injury. Adding to Mr. Dowd's glamour was the fact that he was designing a "ranch house" for us, which I imagined as a sprawling outpost of bunkbeds and hitching posts, with a triangle my mother would ring to call us in from the corral to dinner. It puzzled me that Mr. Dowd and my parents spent so much time discussing something called "the picture window," which was not a term used on any of the ranches I was familiar with.

By the time moving day was upon us, Mr. Dowd had been whittled down to size in my imagination, as had our two-bedroom ranch house, which looked a lot like a cakebox with a low pitched roof and no corral. There was not even a bunkbed, though one would have been convenient since Mike and I had to share a room until Dad could build "the addition." I adjusted quickly, however, to the deflation of my fantasies, happy enough just to be out of that crib, to have a closet that held my clothes instead of me. And I saw immediately that the truly important thing was indeed that picture window.

My mother was utterly transformed the afternoon she walked the mile between 1010 Main Street and the almost-ready new house, carrying a big bottle of Windex and a few sections of the *Chicago Tribune*. Pumping alongside her on my tricycle, I saw my mother pulse and glow with the pleasure of imminent escape. Even her stride was different, longer and faster and hard to keep up with. She was not wearing one of those tight-waisted, broad-shouldered, long-skirted suits that made her look so different from the other mothers in the park, whom my dad called "dowdy." For the first time, she was wearing pants, a brand new kind of pants called "pedal pushers." As I sprayed and she wiped each of the thirty-five small panes of the grand whole that was the picture window, it felt as if we were pulling the blind forever on those dark forties and snapping it wide open on the light-filled fifties.

By keeping my ears open when Mr. Dowd was around, I had gathered that the other most important thing about our new house was that "the space flowed," which meant my mother wouldn't have to be "stuck in the kitchen." I didn't have a firm grasp on this concept until we moved in, and I quickly figured out that I could run around inside the house in an unbroken circle. How this worked was, the kitchen flowed over a partial, half wall into the dining room which flowed through no wall at all into the living room which flowed around a corner into the hall and back into the kitchen again. It didn't take long to race around this circuit, and it didn't work very well as a route of quick getaway from my brother, because sound followed the same path, giving away my exact whereabouts on the circle unless I stood completely still and held my breath.

In theory, our humble ranch was a descendant, at the level of third or fourth poor cousin, of Frank Lloyd Wright's famed Prairie Houses, whose "open plan" liberated space from the tyranny of Victorian boxiness. Rather than trap light and space within rooms that were boxes within boxes, Wright designed houses that, in his words, gave "a sense of the outside coming in and the inside going out." All this coming and going of space was intended to enhance "the

freedom of the individual," which is why, Wright main-
tained, "I have, lifelong, been fighting the pull of the
specious old box." His wall-busting ideal of a house was "a
shelter that hides nothing."

I don't know if Mr. Dowd was a dedicated disciple of
Frank Lloyd Wright, but I do know that my father, who was
raised in a large Victorian house in a small Iowa town where
dancing was against the law, was. When we drove down
Ridge Boulevard, it was not the imposing Gothic churches
he venerated, but a glass-and-poured-concrete behemoth of
a church inspired by The Master himself. Even at the time,
I understood that my father's appreciation of that odd
church, as rare in Evanston as his appreciation of Adlai
Stevenson and modern art, was good news for me. He
wanted us out of the Victorian box, body and spirit. The
fact that some of his escape routes proved to be about as
transporting as Sister Alexine's magic carpet is, well, just
one of those things.

The "liberation of space" sounded like such a good idea
that it took a lot of living in it to expose the crack in its foundation. I couldn't articulate my distress then, but I recently
found the perfect expression of my feeling about spatial flow
in *Home*, Witold Rybczynski's spirited romp through the history of domestic architecture. As if speaking up for the child
I was, he pinpoints the problem with the so-called open
plan: "The space flows, but so also does sight and sound—
not since the Middle Ages have homes offered as little
personal privacy to their inhabitants."

There was a similar price to pay for the picture window, because what it pictured, after all, was us. Drapes

drawn, we were on display, exposed and self-conscious. In homes all up and down the block, this exerted a not-so-subtle pressure upon families to behave like living color versions of the families pictured in that other new window on the world, television. To get offstage and out of earshot, one had to retreat to the bathroom, which was much in demand, or to the semi-privacy of a bedroom, which felt more like banishment than escape. Bedrooms were where you were sent for being bad, which I was seldom discovered to be.

Eventually, fathers fed up with "flow" would look to the basement for privacy—creating those dark, damp, knotty-pine-paneled dungeons called "rec rooms." It was here that we early children of the suburbs developed the Sunday-night addiction that spawned Disneyland, and it was here that we later forged a permanent associative link between budding sexuality and the smell of mildew. By the mid-fifties, however, when rec rooms were pandemic, the open floor plan and the picture window had already left their imprint on family life. If the quality of our upstairs privacy was medieval, the quality of our response to it was pure, contemporary Javanese.

I owe this insight to cultural anthropologist Clifford Geertz, who noticed that in Java, where houses face the street without walls or fences, and where interior rooms have no doors, families erect psychological barriers to do the work of material ones. The Javanese, he says, "speak softly, hide their feelings, and even in the bosom of a Javanese family you have the feeling that you are in the public square and must behave with appropriate decorum. Javanese shut people out with a wall of etiquette (patterns of politeness are very highly developed), with emotional restraint, and with a general lack of candor in both speech and behavior."

An anthropologist observing life at 1703 Cleveland Street could have drawn the same conclusion. For better or worse, the silence, consideration, and restraint cultivated in the cramped quarters at 1010 Main flourished and grew to maturity in the wide open space of our Cleveland Street ranch.

The picture window let in light, but the light did not reach the nooks and crannies of the imagination. Sometimes one needs to be alone with light, and for that I had to be outdoors, where I usually was, often building forts that offered the privacy from adults that the house did not provide. I preferred designing the forts myself, but I usually subcontracted help of various kinds from my best friend Joey Monticello, who lived across the street in the house whose picture window faced ours.

As in many endeavors, materials dictated design, and we were catholic in our choice of materials—dirt, snow, weeds, cardboard, tree limbs, almost anything at hand except scrap lumber from the new houses that were popping up all over the neighborhood. Lumber usually requires hammers, saws, and nails, and I preferred more natural forms of joining. Our most elaborate creation was a series of underground rooms, connected by tunnels, dug out of the rich loamy soil of a nearby weed lot. Each room was a five-foot cube excavated with those small, head-folding army shovels that were used to dig foxholes in World War II, and later given to children as peacetime toys. Joey and I covered the holes with (in this rare instance) scavenged lumber, upon which we laid layers of newspaper, upon which we scooped a thin layer of dirt as camouflage in the hopes of keeping our lair a secret.

Although impressed by its scale, I came to feel this project was misguided. One obvious problem was that this hideaway was underground, and therefore as dank and dark as our rec rooms. Secondly, the ambitiousness of it drew the attention and eventual participation of our older brothers, who started to boss Joey and me around. By the time we had seven connected rooms, with a communications network of tin-can-and-string telephone lines, our parents got wind of what we were up to. After an on-site inspection, they hastily condemned the premises, claiming a concern about cave-ins. When a task force of parents returned with garden shovels to destroy our handiwork, I shared the general outrage at overbearing adult authority, but I was also glad to be rid of this military compound of a fort.

A brainstorm of which I am still proud led to the next—and my all-time favorite—fort. It was made of adult-head-high weeds left rooted to the ground. First, Joey and I rolled around in a section of weeds to mash them into floor matting. This created a vaguely circular clearing about four child-body widths in diameter. Then we selected two tall, unmashed weeds from opposite sides of the clearing, gently bent them toward the center, and tied their tips together to form an arc. We worked our way around the clearing, repeating this bending and tying until we had woven ourselves inside a wondrous green dome. The beauty of this midsummer fort was that it offered both shade and filtered light. The drawbacks were bugs and a propensity to collapse under the slightest rain. But it was easy to rebuild, and I did so many times that summer, even after Joey lost interest in our fragile green world.

I wonder now why I didn't even try to create a world of my own within my bedroom after Mike took up quarters in the new addition. Perhaps its unsparing newness, its featureless expanse of fresh-painted white walls, overwhelmed my capacity to make an imprint. Or perhaps the house itself made me feel there was something wrong about wanting privacy within its thin walls. Everything was so available to the eye and so brightly lit, so seemingly open and without secrets. There was nothing to explore, and nowhere to hide.

Even the furniture offered itself and us up to full view. "Danish modern," it was called—armless chairs and smooth, clean, blond tables whose blank surfaces withheld nothing. After the first look, there were no surprises. On rainy days, I would search through an old desk that had been banished to the basement, a dark, mahogany secretary with deep side drawers and, better yet, a whole row of pigeonholes hidden behind a delicately hinged folding top. Its cache of old pictures and documents seldom changed, but its recesses held at least the possibility of discovery. Upstairs, in the bright light of the picture window, that dark desk would have been out of place.

All signs of age and idiosyncrasy were downstairs, in the rec room, which housed my father's collections of minerals and fossils, his found objects waiting to become sculptures, his watercolors and oils and bottles of India ink. Or in his basement workshop, where he tied flies, polished gems, chiseled stone, carved wood. We were always welcome in his kingdom, which was a good thing, because my father seemed to own all the privacy in the house.

Upstairs at night, my mother and I found our separate spheres in books, usually novels, which we read companionably in the living room, each present but lost to the thrall of other peoples' imaginations. In those evening hours, freed from housework and homework, we enjoyed a separate, simultaneous contentedness that would become my model for mutual well-being. When I was adult, we would send favorite books back and forth, which was another way of being together, separately, but then we would be diminishing rather than creating a measure of distance. We practiced a quiet domesticity upstairs while downstairs my father taught by example the pleasures of engaged solitude. And by his absence, my brother, off to the wider world of St. George High School and then to Harvard, beckoned me to imagine life beyond the ranch.

By day the house became my way station, a safety zone of parental care and watchfulness, to which I returned after spending long hours outside, building and rebuilding those hand-cobbled forts; not long after I had outgrown them, we were in the age of the second car, which functioned as a kind of teenage fort on wheels. When I left for college in faraway Texas, knowing I might never return to Cleveland Street except as a visitor, I felt no tug of regret. Home would always be my parents, but it had never really been that house.

I treated a succession of dorm rooms much as I had my bedroom on Cleveland Street. They were fine for sleeping, but not for much else, and I expended little energy on making them mine. Since I was the out-of-towner (by many hundreds of miles), I usually arrived to a room already decorated by a roommate's mother, my bed selected and under a spread of her choosing. "I hope this is all right, dear," more than one mother said while an embarrassed daughter rolled her eyes. "Here's the receipt." It *was* all right. I didn't care about bedspreads and throw pillows. I cared about books and boys, increasingly in that order.

When I graduated from dorms to apartments, my requirements remained minimal. I wanted plenty of light and quiet and, for unexplored reasons, a patina of age. In Boston and later in New York, I gravitated toward "prewar" buildings, with thick walls and crown molding, with interior doors so substantial and solid they shared no kinship with the hollow-cored slightnesses of the ranch house. These doors didn't seem to be apologizing for interrupting the flow of space past their sills. I appreciated the fortitude of my doors, especially during the years I labored through twelve-hour work days in the unpartitioned frenzy of a newsroom.

Though congenial to my needs, I didn't quite think of these apartments as home. I owned my last Manhattan apartment, but I knew that it, like its rented predecessors, was temporary quarters, a phase, no more lasting than my ill-considered young marriage. I did, however, begin accumulating furnishings I thought of as permanent. I had been introduced to the pecking order of antiques by my southern husband, who had grown up in an antebellum house under continual renovation in Charleston, South Carolina. I never did take to the niceties of the antique hunt, but I developed an appreciation for the previously owned. Bit by bit, I acquired a rolltop desk and a brass bed, a wing chair and Oriental rugs, a settee, a china cabinet, and a variety of small tables of indeterminate pedigree.

Everything I acquired was old, somewhere on the spectrum between antique and used. This was not a matter of budget, or even of a clearly defined aesthetic. It was visceral. I wanted little that was new. This dismayed certain of my friends, who believed period decor was bad for the soul, a harbinger of conservative yearnings that might find their way into my politics. I was as progressive as the next person, I insisted, my attachment to the old notwithstanding.

I wasn't wedded, after all, to any particular period, any self-selected golden age of the home, and I wasn't so far retrenched that I was not a woman of my times, even arguably ahead of it. Why else was I working so hard at pioneering jobs that left me almost no time to spend at "home," where post-, not pre-modern art hung on my thick old walls. I was the first on my block to live under the off-kilter gaze of Cindy Sherman's self[sic]-portraits. And I did not camouflage my television or VCR or computer in a retrofitted credenza. I didn't want the old around me because it allied me to a tradition of circumscribing mores, but because . . . well, because, when it came to furnishings, I just knew what I liked if not precisely why.

When I left Manhattan and moved upstate, I knew my furniture would fit in, but I wasn't so sure about me. After forty years of suburbs and cities, I knew I wanted hills and streams, but was I really suited to a county of farflung villages whose populations had remained in the three or low-four digits for two hundred years? I temporized by renting a furnished house for two years before hiring a moving van to haul my old belongings to their new setting. I had bought a house and intended to make it a home, without quotation marks.

Like all the affordable houses in the area, the house I bought was old, about 120 years old, and in urgent need of renovation. Although the white paint on its two stories of clapboards was dingy and peeling, the exterior was sound in the ways that matter; the serious problems were interior. The wood support posts in the basement had rotted over decades of contact with a damp, dirt floor, causing the upper floors to settle with a pronounced tilt toward the center, as if the floorboards were gravitating toward the pull of an invisible drain. The house needed jacking up, which would cause the cracks in its plaster walls to become chasms. This presented an "opportunity," as my contractor phrased it, to dismantle the walls, rewire, insulate, and, in any other ways I wished, bring the house into the twentieth century.

Only now, nearly ten years after the fact, is it clear that I was guided in almost every wish by an unconscious formed in the darkness of 1010 Main, and reformed in the inescapable brightness of Cleveland Street. I wanted all available light, but I also wanted doors that would open and shut to the fluctuating pulse of my desires for privacy and contact, solitude and sociability. I wanted to control the flow of space rather than be swept, always, into the open by its unchecked force.

Like most American houses built after 1860, my Victorian box had a "balloon frame," which meant, among other things, that its interior walls did not support the basic structure of the house and so could be removed or rearranged pretty much at will. When it was built, and when I became its third owner, the house was divided into ten rooms, which was considerably more than I needed or could imagine separate uses for. And one unfortunate result of walling off so many rooms was that daylight could only enter most of them from one direction. Easterly rooms full of sunlight in the morning were emptied of it by afternoon, when the westerly rooms suddenly perked up after a long dim morning. The goal I set myself was providing each room with plentiful natural light without opening up the space so much that it ran wild through the house.

To this end I removed walls and added windows, turning ten dark boxes into seven light-exposed but still private rooms. The solution I discovered was to calculate carefully the placement of windows in relation to doors. With its door closed, each room now had at least two exposures; an open door let in light from a third or fourth direction. If the house was full of guests, this sometimes entailed a small compromise with privacy, but not often, because the doors opened onto a light-flooded foyer rather than onto another room likely to be in use.

In the sociable downstairs rooms—living, dining, and kitchen—I removed doors and one wall to increase light and reduce boxiness. I left the door on my downstairs study and doubled its window to approximate the light from, yes, a picture window. But this was a rear window, facing west toward yard and garden and woods; the only displaying it fostered was between me and the birds. Upstairs, I turned five bedrooms into three larger ones, capacious enough to become worlds of their own. One of the original bedrooms was so small and dim that I converted it to a closet. Only years later did I realize that this turnabout was my best revenge upon 1010 Main.

Recognitions were delayed, the particulars of my agenda hidden, in part because I worked hastily to turn house into home. The year I bought the house, my mother was ill, and I divided my time, in unpredictable sequences and proportions, between shoring up the foundation of my new life and witnessing the gradual destruction of the first life I'd known. Most of my decisions of every kind that year were based on instinct and urgency. I knew that my sudden desire to create a home was linked by more than circumstance to the sudden likelihood of my mother's death. I was aware that whenever I left New York to join my parents, I said I was flying "home," and that whenever I returned to New York, I also said I was flying "home." In neither direction did home mean a structure.

My home away from home was my parents, not their ranch house, nor their neighborhood, nor their suburb, which by this time no longer existed in relation to Chicago but to Minneapolis. To prolong my father's career, they had moved to Minnesota almost fifteen years earlier, depriving me of the vicarious continuity I had counted on in many ways. If our spirit of connectedness had a locus now, it was not in Minnesota or Illinois or New York, but in Italy, where we had found our kindredness as three adults traveling together on splendid but neutral terrain. As long as my parents lived, home could be a shifting site. In a world minus them, I would need to fix myself in place.

Timing determined that the place would be this house, whose collapse I could forestall, whose existence I could insure, barring catastrophic acts of God and nature, beyond my own. As I worked to give the house a second life, I knew the general nature of my investment, but only time revealed to me how many of my specific decisions about space and light had their source in my earliest, unarticulated intuitions about what might have eased the strains upon our postwar foursome.

Not much later, when my father's and then my brother's deaths followed far too closely in the wake of my mother's, the source of my attachment to the old came into clearer focus. From sometime early in my adulthood, I had wanted to live among reminders of a history that preceded me, among furnishings that bore silent witness to the erasures underlaying the tabula rasa of my suburban youth. I wanted to escape the tyranny of the ahistorical new, which disguises itself as a timeless normalcy.

I had come to believe that we children of the early postwar suburbs had been the target of a benign but misguided conspiracy, hatched by parents who wanted to close the curtain on a painful past, who wanted to spare their children any deep knowledge of depression and war. And in doing so they also kept us ignorant of the tangled histories they had left behind in the small towns and farms they had forsaken to find work or wage war and, that accomplished, to invent suburbs. By their reckoning, everything before the suburbs was ancient history; before August 1945, prehistory. By their reckoning, I was born the week the world began. Is it any wonder the generation born in America after the war thinks it invented peace and the wheel?

And arriving late, if at all, to an understanding of where we came from, we were slow as well to grasp where we are headed. Since early adulthood I have wanted to be surrounded by reminders of the history that preceded me. Now I want as well to live among signs of what will outlast me. The house in Ancram is my place in the continuum. I don't have any illusion that I belong here above all places, or that this house is truly mine; I am its caretaker for an indefinite period, living like all its previous occupants on borrowed time. I have scraped the peeling paint from its clapboards, but I did not sand the house smooth before adding a new coat of color. The wrinkles of time are visible in its alligator skin, and I like it like that. I hope whoever scrapes at the remnants of my labor will, too.

NAMES

ANCRAM IS A place where nothing much happens. What does happen is occasioned by elemental forces, like weather and love. And until you have gone through many turns of those cycles, you remain on the outer rim of awareness here. No matter how long we newcomers stay, if this was a place we chose rather than were born to, we just don't count very much. Our stories don't go back far enough. We may set roots that spread just under the surface, linking newcomer to newcomer, but we have no taproots. We may be occasional objects of curiosity, a source of amusement or irritation, but not of real animosity or joy. Deeper feelings are reserved for those whose latest chapters add small accretions to a long-running serial of feuding and marrying and grieving.

Some newcomers try to butt heads with this indifference, court and curry, and think fifteen or twenty years ought to be enough to matter. Personally, I prefer counting for little. It leaves more room for elective affinities and for solitude. It also makes for tolerance. It is hard to offend or give scandal when no one cares or expects much of you. All that's hoped of a newcomer to Ancram is that he will be a good neighbor, which means that he will behave well when weather happens, that he'll know when to share his water or shovel or electricity, and that he'll know enough to wait his turn.

After a couple years of sharing shovels, some of the ones who were born here might start to get to know your name. But it's more likely that you'll be known by an evolving set of identifying labels, like "the lady who bought Mary Jane's house," then "the lady who bought Mary Jane's house who has the cat with the arrow," then "the lady who painted Mary Jane's house gray, who has the big yellow cat, who fishes," then "the lady who lives in the gray house with the big yellow cat, who fishes and writes about it." When the string of phrases gets too long, you get a name, and you hope it is one you would want to answer to. After ten years, my name has spread a little ways through town, but not far.

I like the slow process of becoming known here, much the way I like days like today when the only thing happening is the weather. It makes me think about what it means to be known by name, and what it takes to recognize when something is happening. This morning, for instance, I was reading by the window in my study when I was distracted by a flicker of movement in my peripheral vision. A bird. There was a time when that would have been the end of the story, unless perhaps the bird had been bright red or yellow or exhibited some other striking feature that pulled it from the periphery to the center of my attention. In that case I might have risen from my chair, gone to another room to fetch my binoculars, and returned to discover the bird had not bothered to wait for me.

These days, I seldom need my binoculars, because even without catching clear sight of a bird, even if it is just an average-sized, brownish-grayish blur in the distance, I can often tell what kind of bird it is. Without really trying, I've become familiar with other clues: a sound, the shape of a flight path, the degree of flittiness or calm, or of sociability—whether it flies alone, paired, or in a flock. So this morning when I looked up from my reading, my brain registered "dark bird, about size of robin, feeding on ground, flock nearby, kind of chunky," and I thought, "It's mid-March, and didn't I notice the pale green tips of daylilies poking up through the unmelted snow and road grit at the end of the driveway?" Bingo. The string of phrases coalesced into a name—cowbird. A drab female, just this moment arriving in my backyard after a winter down South.

Last summer, I achieved my personal best at long-distance bird identification. I was sitting on my friend and neighbor David Barnes's deck with a gathering of visitors from the city when someone spotted a hawk and a smaller bird perched together on a treetop about one hundred yards away. Jumping to a logical conclusion, the visitor said, "Look, a hawk and its young!" I looked. The hawk was clearly a hawk. The identification of the smaller bird could only be a guess from our distance. All I could see was its general shape, but the smaller bird was heavier headed than the hawk. A hawk and a kingfisher, I guessed, knowing both were likely in the vicinity, although I don't think of hawks as particularly companionable birds, especially to other species. David's binoculars proved me right, which led me to speculate that perhaps hawks and kingfishers can perch peaceably side by side, because they keep an eye out for different prey. While the hawk scans the field for rodents, the kingfisher keeps his eye on the pond.

Why is the slow accretion of such knowledge so satisfying to me? It's not the sheer stockpiling of information that pleases me, but the ability to recognize what is before my eyes, to see not just small grayish birds but titmice and juncoes and flycatchers. Not just trees, but oaks and maples and cherries and elms; not just oaks, but white oaks and black oaks and scarlet oaks, recognizable not just in summer by their leaves but in winter, too, by differences in their barks and their branching patterns. It's not a know-it-all kind of thing. I don't go about telling the names of birds and trees and wildflowers unless I'm asked. I remember very well how tedious I found such unsolicited tutoring when, years ago, my father prematurely tried to make me his student.

Nor am I a person who is compulsive about drawing distinctions. I don't bother, never have, to notice the make or model of a car; I'm content for them to be a blur of red or blue or white on wheels. I have intended for years to be more attentive to the varieties and vintages of wines; the information never sticks. The classification of rocks and minerals still bores me. But the naming of birds and plants strikes another chord. It makes me feel I am unraveling a deep mystery bit by bit. A mystery of place. The knowledge feels intimate, not abstract, as if I were getting to know the neighbors, which I am.

City people—by which I mean people who, no matter where they live, need the unmistakable stimulus of plentiful choice and hurried action—are prone to see nature as a backdrop, and so, of course, they are quickly bored by it. They keep waiting, as I once did, for the play to begin. But in Ancram, nature is not the backdrop, it's the show, and knowing the cast is essential to following the action. The difference in naming is a difference in seeing. Seeing a chunky dark bird on March 16 is not the same as seeing the first cowbird return to your yard on his migration north. The name tells me it is spring, that a promise has been kept, that a story is still unfolding.

Yesterday, July 14, I was returning from the stream about eight in the evening, having caught not fish but the rare sight of two foxes playing at the edge of the water. As I walked home along the dirt road that runs between the cemetery and the town park, eager to tell whoever would listen about the foxes, about their long, bushy, white-tipped tails, about how they leaped and tumbled over one another like kittens, about how close they had let me come, about how I had looked for and found two fox holes on the bank, as I was replaying all this in my mind in preparation for a telling, I noticed that a large patch of milkweed was growing on the ridge just in

front of the new basketball court. Two minutes later, I was
hailing a friend I saw exiting The Little Store, insisting she
come see the patch of milkweed that was growing where
David Boice and his crew had cleared the brambles to expand
the basketball court. In my excitement over the milkweed, I
forgot even to mention the foxes.

Why was I more excited about a patch of common
milkweed, a plant whose silky burst pods and oozing white
sap I had taken for granted since childhood, than about seeing foxes, creatures I had never encountered on foot before
in my life? Because the presence of milkweed meant that
monarch larvae, which feed only on milkweed foliage,
might be growing into caterpillars there. And monarch butterflies, usually as reliable a sign of summer as robins and
fireflies, had been mysteriously absent from the Northeast
for the previous two summers. I had felt their absence from
my backyard the first summer without realizing the loss was
more than personal, and more than local. In the fall, I read
that the researchers who count monarchs as they head south
on their migration routes recorded a 90 percent reduction in
the eastern monarch population; in the Northeast, almost
none had been spotted during that summer of 1992.

Seeing that milkweed patch, I knew that if the monarchs were making a comeback in Ancram, the evidence
would be found there. After I had stashed my fishing gear
and returned to the park, there was little to see in the fading
light. But today, when I checked, there were a dozen young
monarchs flitting in the milkweed, as well as several other
species of butterfly whose names and stories I do not know.
I knew that most monarchs have a natural lifespan of only

two or three weeks, but that these monarchs, achieving their wings in July, were the special generation. They were the long-lived monarchs that would leave Ancram in a month or so to begin a two-thousand-mile flight to certain specific mountain enclaves in south-central Mexico, where they would convene with the other millions of their generation born east of the Rockies. Their arrival in Mexico would be celebrated, as it has been since pre-Columbian times, by religious ceremonies honoring the butterflies as the return-ing souls of the dead. Throughout the winter, monarchs would cloak the fir trees so densely that whole mountain-sides would bloom orange and black.

All this was new knowledge to me, and it made the dif-ference in what I saw among those weeds. I saw the milk-weed's dusty-pink flower heads and a small stand of young sumac nearby, which I feared might invade and overwhelm the milkweed by next year. I saw the boundary line of the power mower's realm, and reminded myself to call David Boice and ask him not to cut the patch down. I saw large yel-low-and-black butterflies, monarch look-alikes in their stained-glass patterning, and I noticed for the first time how different their lazy flight pattern is from the restive monarch's. I saw black butterflies with orange markings, a color negative of the monarch, flying low and nearly crash-ing into my legs. I wondered if there was a reason why all the butterflies in the milkweed patch bore a resemblance to the monarch—either as its imitator or its negative?

That patch, which might have fallen easily beneath my notice, was full of action, abuzz with myth and marvel, link-ing me to distant cultures and to my first home, where I had learned the first fact that was now drawn into a much larger web. As children, we were fascinated by the information, impressed upon us by parents, that the white ooze of milkweed was poisonous; we were thrilled by the threat of mortal danger so close. Now I know the milk we lived in delicious fear of is the milk that keeps monarchs safe; birds are so sickened by their first toxic taste that they are never tempted by those gaudy wings again. And I know, because my neighbor Nora, born in Ancram, told me so, that there have never been religious observances for monarchs here, but it has been customary in her family for generations to give names to monarchs. Tending their vegetable garden, Nora might see a monarch wafting by and say to her husband, Sherwood, "Charlie's back," meaning Uncle Charlie, who died last winter.

I have probably arrived too late in Ancram for anyone ever to call a monarch by my name, but I am as pleased as Nora when I see one in my garden. The annual return of the monarch, like the return of the cowbirds and the predictable sequence of perennials blooming in my garden, are the elements of an evolving new calendar by which I chart my days. It is a welcome evolution, allowing me to overlay the year's cycle of haunting dates with a new cycle of anniversaries. Most anniversaries originate as celebrations of beginnings, but devolve over time into commemorations of endings. When the bee balm blooms, when the bluebirds come looking for nesting boxes, when the tree frogs leave the pond and head for the woods—I am glad to have this growing set of replenishing associations. Named and storied, like the saints whose lives turn on the wheel of the liturgical year, the cowbird, the monarch, and the milkweed intercede for me.

T I M E

"You're as old as you feel." — Beatrice Schreiber

"In the woods is perpetual youth." — Ralph Waldo Emerson

*"The distinction between past, present
and future is only an illusion,
even if a stubborn one."* — Albert Einstein

―WHENEVER SHE WAS asked
about her age, no matter the source or circumstances of the
question, whether arising from her curious daughter or a
hospital administrator after her medical history, my mother
would answer, "You're as old as you feel." Firmer pressure
only brought a firmer response: "It's none of your business."
Once, pressed by an unswervable nurse on the eve of major
surgery, she banished everybody but her tormentor from the

room before yielding the answer, which in any case was probably not true.

As a child, I suspected my mother took this stance, so untypical of her in its rigidity, because she, like all her nine brothers and sisters, had prematurely gray hair. Often presumed for this reason to be older than she was, she was, I guessed, too proud to protest her youthfulness. I had to revise that theory when it became clear that, although gray-headed in their twenties, my mother and her siblings were all to be compensated in later years by looking, in every other respect, at least a decade younger than their years.

As a teenager, I attributed her reticence about age to another species of vanity, this one provoked by the fact that she was older than my father, by two years I think, but, of course, I can't be sure, either of her age or of her motivation, about which she was equally unforthcoming. "Oh, I don't know," was her unfailing response to the question of why she wouldn't answer the question. In time, my father assumed the same no-comment position toward the age question, although not with the same unassailable conviction. After all, he had age-based qualifications for pensions and early retirement and Social Security to factor into his principles. When I asked him why he thought my mother was so committed to agelessness, he said, "Well, it's probably just that so many people have preconceptions about what it means to be a certain age that it can skew the way they think of you—even the way you think of yourself. She just prefers not to tell."

That made sense to me, particularly as I got older myself. I might, for instance, be climbing a tree, just because it was there in the woods where I was walking alone, and its branches, arrayed just so, seemed to issue an invitation. Maybe fifteen feet up, I would pause to survey my next choice of rungs and while plotting my strategy be waylaid by the thought, "I'm forty . . . or forty-five . . . or a half season from fifty. When am I going to stop doing this?" I would remember how it felt to climb a tree as a girl, and remember as well how amazed that girl would have been to know she would still be climbing trees at fifty, how incomprehensible the very idea of *being* fifty was to her.

This pause, into which reflection rushed when only strategy was wanted, changed everything. When I began climbing, I was ageless, by which I mean I experienced my encounter with the tree only as quintessential self-stuff acting on impulse toward a pleasure it was perfectly capable of attaining. Then suddenly I was out on a limb, stranded somewhere between twelve and fifty, urged upward and downward by perverse and conflicting impulses that had nothing left in them of unself-conscious pleasure seeking. On the upside was the desire to prove I can still climb, the hope that curiosity and sensation can triumph over self-consciousness; on the downside was the fear of falling on aging bones, the fear of looking foolish (although who's looking?), or worse, looking quaintly doughty, and the sinking feeling that it is too late. Not too late to climb trees, but too late to climb them on impulse unimpeded by reflection. The solution, it seemed, was to get my reflections in sync with my impulses. But how?

I have reached that impasse—in the crook of a tree, on the slippery stones of a fast-rushing stream, on the frozen surface of a lake that groans and rumbles under the slice of my skates—many times in the last ten years. Each time, as I try to disentangle wise caution from foolish constriction, I have recalled a singular moment of my girlhood, one that felt for many years like the last moment of my girlhood. It was a Sunday morning, and I was twelve, only minutes home from church and already changed into jeans, eager to get the muscle memory of kneeling out of my legs. My father, who regularly abstained from church, was sitting at the dining-room table sipping coffee and reading the newspaper. Before heading outside for the afternoon, I rushed up to him on impulse, assumed a flex-kneed fighting crouch, raised my fists, and said, "Put up your dukes," the usual preliminary to brief bouts of shadowboxing as commonplace between us as good-night kisses.

In the flash of time it took him to put up his dukes, I had put mine down. From nowhere, from out the unclouded skies of girlhood, a lightning bolt of adolescent self-consciousness had struck a powerful blow, below the belt and chastening to the core. I knew in that instant that I was too old to shadowbox with my father. I was twelve, I menstruated; the chain running round my neck and beneath my shirt held not a St. Christopher's medal, as my parents believed, but a dogtag signifying I went steady with Carl Volante; I had just changed into jeans from nylons, garter belt, and high heels. I had to choose—garter belt or shadowboxing? Silently, I made my choice, while my father waited, dukes still up, for the round that would never happen. I don't know why the bell rang in my head at that precise instant, but it did, sending me back to my corner for more years than I had yet lived.

In time I would realize the sad folly of the choices I made in the name of becoming a woman, 1950s American model, which I then regarded as a subspecie aeternitatis. There were prices to pay for those needless constrictions, not the least of which was a certain artificiality that entered my relationship with my father from the moment I put my dukes down. Decades later, out on a limb, feeling a similar tug of choice, I didn't want to set myself up for similar regrets. Why wait for hindsight to reprove me for constricting my behavior in the name of age as I once had in the name of sex? Since both my parents had died by the time I was forty-three, I couldn't put the question to them, but I knew what my mother would say: "You're as old as you feel." Perhaps there had been more truth than evasion in her reply.

The problem, of course, was, how old did I feel? Some days, in some circumstances, I felt twelve. Often, as Ralph Waldo Emerson predicted, the circumstances were woodsy but the youth I found there was not perpetual. Perhaps if I could just stand still in Nature, letting myself become like Emerson, "a transparent eyeball," seeing all while "the currents of the Universal Being circulate through me." But I preferred to move, and then a stumble, a turned ankle, or even just a steep uphill climb could make all the years of my life rush back in the blink of a sweat-blurred eye. Lakes contained a more reliable elixir than woods. I was a better swimmer at forty-five than I had ever been before, and in the soft, mineral-laden water of a nearby lake, not just years but time itself seemed to vanish as I braided strands of silken water and self and air together stroke after even stroke.

The summer after my brother died, I spent a lot of time in that lake. His death at age fifty had removed the benign aura of abstraction from the contemplation of my own mortality. That summer, my forty-sixth, I was beset by perplexities that arose not only from my known distance from birth but also from my unknown proximity to death, whose reality was as vivid to me as my own flesh. I didn't want my innocence back, any more than I wanted to be twelve again, but I didn't want the mortal coil wound so tight around me that I stopped taking deep breaths of the life still in me. Swimming, often alone and far from shore, I had to take deep breaths, and my reward was to feel those coils slip from me and dissolve in the water like a dream in morning light.

Sometimes, in the amber light that suffused my closed eyelids as I swam, an image would rise slowly through the water toward me, achieving an exquisite clarity as it came near to linger a moment before drifting away; the image was always a face, of either my mother or father or brother, as they had looked in health, and the faces brought with them a feeling of reconnection unavailable to me then through more deliberate efforts of memory. As pleased as I was by these images, I did not try to court or capture them. Over the years I had learned that consolation cannot be coerced, and so I took my solace when and where it came, with gratitude.

Once, while resting on the dock after a late afternoon swim, I looked into the water and saw an image that sent waves of pure bliss washing over my brain. In the still, glassy surface of the water, I saw the reflection of my face and right shoulder, so preternaturally clear that the reflection seemed to contain more reality than its source; swimming back and forth through the still image, without rippling it, was a school of small bluegills. The effect was like that of certain Escher drawings, with the images of self and fish alternately coming in and out of focus, and for split seconds existing simultaneously and inextricably.

I don't know why the vision of fish swimming through my head should provoke such delight, unless it was the rarity of seeing the confluence of self and world made visible. Or perhaps the pleasure arose from seeing certain literary associations turned inside out, the image of fish swimming not through a skull resting in its watery grave, but through the reflection of my living flesh. I wondered at the image and my response to it, but that did not stop me from accepting it, like the faces that drifted toward me from the deep, as a gift.

The lake was generous to me that summer, which is why I continued swimming well into October before facing the fact that the sensation of ecstatic well-being that followed the sensation of diving into a pool of freeze-dried needles was a symptom of midstage hypothermia. Reluctantly, I left the lake that had quieted my concerns about age and mortality, not by inducing a state of perpetual youth but by submerging me in a subjective state of time out of time. The lake had been my medium for entering a waking dream that intimated answers that evaporated on land. No amount of rational thought or borrowed faith, no amount of thinking, wishing, or bargaining with the gods of good deeds, hard work, and healthy living brought the peace of mind the lake had bestowed without my even asking.

What got me through that winter was a dream. I dreamed that I was taking a leisurely Sunday drive down a dirt road through a slightly rolling landscape of wheat fields in what I somehow knew was central Iowa. It was afternoon on a clear summer day, and everything was lit by a soft golden light. There was something out of the ordinary about the landscape, but I couldn't quite figure out what until I noticed how pristine it was. There were no power lines or motorized farm machines in sight, no billboards or road signs of any kind. As I rounded a gentle curve in the road, I saw a redheaded boy with a fishing pole over his shoulder walking toward me in the distance. Drawing closer, I saw that the boy was dressed in knickers and kneesocks, and that he was in fact my father as I had seen him looking in pictures from his Iowa boyhood. It didn't seem the least bit strange to me that my father walked as a boy through the landscape of his 1920s youth while I drove slowly toward him in a 1990 Honda.

When we came abreast, I stopped the car to greet my father, and he gestured that I should turn the car around and follow him. Pausing briefly at the car window, he said he had found a great new fishing hole, by the bridge just a little ways back, about a ten-minute walk beyond the curve I had just rounded. By the time I had turned the car around, he was out of sight; I figured he had taken a shortcut through the fields, but I knew I could catch up with him at the fishing hole. Approaching the bridge, I was surprised and disappointed to see that cars of every vintage lined both sides of the road for quite a distance. Mobs of people—men, women, and children—were gathering along both banks of the stream. What on earth did my father think was so great about a stretch of stream that looked like a carnival midway? And how was I going to find him in this crush of people?

I parked and joined the crowd parading several abreast up the near bank of the stream, which was lined by large trees whose branches formed a canopy over our heads. A meadow lined the far bank. A short ways ahead, a huge, bulging throng of people had stopped to pluck something from the trees, filling bags and baskets and aprons. When I became part of the bulge, I looked up and saw the trees were laden with mushrooms—beautiful, shining, obviously magic mushrooms. My excitement over the magic mushrooms quickly turned to dismay. There were so many people and they were each picking so many mushrooms, there might not be any left for me by the time I was in position to grab one. I was starting to feel frantic and angry at the prospect of missing my share when it suddenly became apparent to me that part of the magic of these mushrooms was that there would always be plenty for everyone. These were the loaves and fishes of mushrooms. With this awareness I became calm, and I was able to see that this was a genial and welcoming mob.

When I had picked my fill, I walked a little farther upstream to a less crowded stretch of bank where I thought I might have a better chance of finding my father. I kept walking upstream until finally I saw him ahead on the other bank. He was fishing with a little dark-haired girl, about six years old, and when I hollered over to them, they both looked up, and I saw that the little girl was me, and that she/I was my father's sister. We waved and smiled at one another, and I felt a serene bliss that ushered me into wakefulness.

Awake, I knew at once that I had the answer to a riddle that had preoccupied me in childhood: What age are people in heaven? I had asked the question of nuns, priests, my mother, but never my father, because he wasn't a Catholic and so couldn't be expected to know about such things. Some guessed you were the age at which you died. Others guessed you could be whatever age you wanted to be. The only firm answer came from Sister Stella, who said everyone in heaven was thirty-three, because that was Christ's age at his death and therefore it was the perfect age—just as six feet was the perfect height, exactly achieved by the mature Christ and by no mortal before or since, all of whom erred by at least a millimeter in one direction or the other. (Though Sister Stella cited no sources, I now know her certitude came from St. Augustine, who in *The City of God* discusses the age of resurrected bodies as well as the related issues of the height, weight, and likely length of heavenly hair and fingernails.)

None of the answers, firm or speculative, satisfied me, because the only thing I knew for sure about heaven was that you were supposed to be perfectly happy there, and how could you be happy if everyone was old or everyone was thirty-three or even if everyone was whatever age they wanted to be, which would only lead to conflicts of celestial interest? What if, like me, you wanted to be a child to your mother, who might want to be a child to her mother, who might want . . . ad infinitum? Depending on the pecking order for wish-granting, you might end up being older than your grandmother. Or what would happen if I died as a child and my brother died as an old man—how could we play together in heaven?

The dream had given me a vision of a heaven I could embrace. We could be all ages, if not simultaneously, in infinite sequence and permutations. I could be age to my father's youth, youth to his age; I could be his daughter, his mother, his sister. For every variation in our relative ages, there were roles that allowed their enactment, and each of the roles was satisfying because each contained a variant of the pleasure that existed in the actual, experienced bond of the two human beings who had known and loved one another on earth. The reversals, exchanges, and general flexibility of roles my parents and I had learned to enjoy in the last years of their lives would each have their bodily equivalents, a physical plasticity to match the subtlety and range of emotional variations. This imagined heaven, unlike "the eternal mass" often upheld by the nuns as the ultimate reward for good children, would not be boring.

The only problem was, this answer to the riddle of heaven had come to me when I no longer believed in heaven—or hell or that most likely of destinations, purgatory. But then, why was I, in the waking hours of the days and weeks and months that followed that dream, so pleased by its recollection? With the dream had come a conviction that it contained a truth to be found in some dimension of reality. It didn't matter whether it was a truth of religion or imagination or physics. Nor did it matter that the dimension was not one I could routinely experience, unless, perhaps, I dedicated my life to one of the myriad meditative disciplines of Eastern mysticism. Besides, in that case, the heaven I envisioned would probably turn out to be just some lower way station on the road to nirvana, and I might find myself on an express that didn't stop there. I might be expected to keep traveling until I had lost all sense of individual consciousness, and that prospect appealed to me about as much as an eternal mass.

If I wanted to explore an arena of knowledge in which my intuitions might find reinforcement, Einsteinian space-time, of which I had only the fuzziest understanding, seemed to hold more promise. So when the allure of the mushroom dream had demonstrated its staying power over several seasons, I decided to pick up a dropped stitch of my education. Though scientifically literate (I had even enrolled in my university's school of science and engineering), I had always hated physics, which I associated with rolling balls and pulley experiments. In high school, all the more interesting questions had been answered with "because God made it that way," and in college, physics was "applied" with a vengeance to the building of bridges, not castles in the air. Classical physics—i.e., Newton's physics—had been erected as the gateway to Einstein's space-time, and it never occurred to me that I could just hop the fence.

Or maybe I just lacked the motivation to find the universe where, in Einstein's words, "The distinction between past, present and future is only an illusion, even if a stubborn one." Now I was ready to explore, and I took as my guide Paul Davies, the Australian natural philosopher whose books on cosmology, relativity theory, and particle physics were reputed (reliably) to be both lucid and unimpeachably informed. Davies's footnotes and indices led me to other "new" physicists, and soon I was traveling in the heady company of those who live daily with the knowledge that there is no absolute distinction between space and time, energy and matter, existence and nonexistence. Reading their works was at first a bit like looking at the bluegills swimming through my reflection, with fish and face alternating as figure and ground. Nose in the book, I was spirited off to realms of the cosmically large and the subatomically small, where up may as well be down and often is. Nose out of the book, I plummeted back to what some physicists call "the zone of middle dimensions"—i.e., the realm of daily experience where we content ourselves with the evidence of our senses.

I liked learning that, theoretically, if I could travel in a rocket ship at a velocity approaching the speed of light, I might reach some distant coordinate in space-time where it made sense for me to be my father's sister. Or to be more precise, I might reach a coordinate in space-time where, if I had a powerful enough telescope, I could look back at earth and see my father in his boyhood, while somebody else speeding away from both me and earth toward some third coordinate might see my father as a boy and me as a girl, not to mention the whole spectrum of other possible relative ages, depending on our relative velocities and distances.

According to relativity theory, as I understand it, which is imperfectly, no amount of whizzing around in space-time would bring my father and me together in one place at these variable ages. In fact, since my speed would have slowed the flow of time in my rocket ship relative to earth-time, when I returned from the distance that allowed me to perceive my father as a boy, I would find he had aged vastly more than I did in the interval. But that glitch didn't bother me. I wasn't looking for confirmation of the literal possibilities of the mushroom dream. I'm not crazy, and since I typically move at a velocity considerably slower than the speed of light, the issue was moot, anyway. What mattered to me was discov-

ering that, in the farthest reaches of theoretical and experi-
mental physics, time is immensely more flexible than we are
accustomed to thinking.

I found it reassuring to learn that in Einstein's universe,
there is no absolute, universal "now," just an infinite range of
possible vantage points in space-time; whatever sliver of
space-time we subjectively experience as happening "now" is
only a by-product of our location in the universe, influenced
by our motion relative to every other location in the universe. When we look into the sky, we are looking into the
past; feeling its warmth on my face, I look up and see the sun
as it was eight minutes ago. "Unless you are a solipsist," Paul
Davies writes in my favorite passage from *About Time: Einstein's
Unfinished Revolution*, "there is only one rational conclusion to
draw from the relative nature of simultaneity: events in the
past and future have to be every bit as real as events in the
present. In fact, the very division of time into past, present
and future seems to be physically meaningless."

This theoretically inescapable conclusion—that all
events from all of time exist all at once in the timescape of
the universe—is what underlies Einstein's statement about
our stubborn propensity to dissect time into illusory tenses.
What occasioned his writing those words in a letter was a
desire to console the widow of his good friend Michele
Besso, whose death in earth-time happened only a few
weeks before Einstein's own. Even for Einstein, however, the
solace of space-time was limited. A few days closer to his
own death in 1955, Einstein confided to a friend that he too
had trouble shaking off the grip of the illusory present.
According to his friend, the philosopher Rudolf Carnap,

Einstein admitted he felt there was "something essential about the now," even though he still believed its reality lay "just outside the realm of science."

Though he had revolutionized physics by claiming the entire universe as a province of his mind, Einstein remained inescapably a son of Newton, the father of earth-time, of "absolute, true and mathematical time," which stops for no man, but "of itself, and from its own nature, flows equably without relation to anything external." Those firm words, from the preface of Newton's *Principia* (1687), ushered in the reign of modern clock-time, which marches, tick by tock, irreversible, unstoppable, relentlessly predictable. Clock-time, the fundament of classical physics and social efficiency, makes the schedule, and the train that runs on it. It enforces the law of one, universal "now," and if you don't hop to it, the train will pass you by. The past is gone forever, and the future doesn't exist.

Until Einstein, Newton's *Principia* was considered the last word on time, as infallible as if spoken ex cathedra by the father of "the one, true, holy, apostolic church." Though on cosmic and subatomic scales it has proved to be a limited and provincial conception, Newton's clockwork universe is still considered the domain of common sense. And though more comprehensively true, Einstein's flexible cosmos, with its warps and woofs of expanding and contracting time, is often described as "counterintuitive." But is it really? Was the moron who threw the clock out the window an idiot savant? Don't we all know that time can speed up and slow down and even threaten to stand still? I am personally acquainted with a phenomenon I call "mall warp," in which five hours of clock-time vanish when I have only had one hour of lived experience. Perhaps the irony is that for three hundred years we have been raised from the cradle to dismiss our most scientifically astute intuitions as being "just outside the realm of science"?

The first two things I remember being taught by my mother, in a deliberative let's-sit-down-and-get-this-straight fashion, were how to tell time and say the "Hail, Mary." In memory, I am about four when I ask my mother to explain what she sees when she looks at the big black-and-white circle hanging high up on the kitchen wall. I must have understood time before she taught me how to tell it, though, because I did not just learn to memorize the names for the various positions of the "hands" that morning. I immediately related the movement of the hands to the events of a day— to when my brother would come home from school, my father from work, to dinnertime and bedtime, to the division of experience into predictable units of routine. Surprised and pleased that I understood the clock lesson so easily, my mother decided I was ready to learn something else as well. That night, at bedtime, she taught me how to ask Holy Mary, Mother of God, to pray for us, "now and at the hour of our death. Amen."

I wonder now if my mother knew how profound and lasting a lesson she was teaching. That day I learned not only about the division of time into hours and minutes but also the division of time from eternity, science from religion, objectivity from subjectivity. At the age of four, I became a full-fledged member of Western civilization. Did my mother know it would take so many decades, and the hour of her death, for me to begin learning again? Confronting the riddle of time anew, I am glad she also taught me the first line of her gnostic gospel: "You're as old as you feel."

And what a splendid, saving irony that my father, named Newton after Sir Isaac, should appear to me in a dream as Father Time, not in the guise of a gray-bearded old man with his scythe, but as a redheaded boy with his fishing rod. When I first awoke from that dream I wasn't sure whether time was the river or the far bank; now I think it is both. In the zone of middle dimensions, time flows like a river through pools and eddies and rapids, speeding up and slowing down, curving and circling, but always finally heading in the same direction. But in the vastness of all that is, time exists as it did on the far bank of my dream, as shifting and pliant as memory and imagination. I released my father's ashes into the river, and he returned as a boy to show me what time looks like from his side of the bank. He taught me to appreciate a new kind of time, its sweeping arcs no longer bound to the pendulum of his namesake.

This spring, my fiftieth, I went to the stream with my fly rod about six o'clock one evening and stayed late; everything seemed fresh, reborn, eager to stretch and soar and splash after a long winter's sleep. The trout were jumping with abandon; the beavers were enjoying their newly deepened pool, cruising and diving and slapping their tails to make the water thunder; the great blue heron unfolded his full length, letting his feet drag through the clear blue sky overhead. At dusk, I walked toward home through a hatch of mayflies, a shimmering amber cloud of insects rising from the stream, their delicate double wings and long tails fluttering so fast they looked like tiny spinning tops as they orbited around each other in an upward spiral. I couldn't see the dimension of the hatch while I was in it, but when I stepped nearer to the bank, I saw them hovering above the stream for as far as I could see like an amber milky way.

While I watched, the mayflies (order Ephemeroptera), who achieve maturity the instant they emerge winged from the water, danced closer and closer to the end of their brief lives. But how much time had elapsed for them, spinning through their lives at high velocity, and for me, standing still and entranced? There is a precise mathematical formula, factoring body size and speed of metabolism, that could tell me the exact ratio of difference in our internal clocks. The ratio changed and time shifted when I moved, pressing upstream against the force of the insistently down-rushing stream, and it shifted again when I stumbled, returning me to my years and sending me home with the sprained left hand with which I am now typing. By my calculations, whatever our relative movements, the mayflies and I both belong to the order Ephemeroptera. But I choose to believe that at birth and at death, and at certain unpredictable moments in between, something in us moves close to the speed of light, time dilates, and the moment becomes eternity.

TERRITORY

⟶ NOT TOO LONG ago, I began teaching a class one day a week, on Wednesdays, to graduate students in Columbia University's writing program. The classroom we meet in has one large, light-grabbing window, and I exercise my professorial authority by taking a chair at the head of the table facing it. For two to three hours after class, however, I meet individually with students in a small, windowless box of an office. My lust for light is a matter of record, both written and oral, and the course administrator, who is very knowledgeable about all sorts of records, had arranged for my use of an adjacent sunlit office assigned to a poet who takes Wednesdays off. When she presented me this option, I felt like a reprieved inmate, until I opened the door and took my heliotropic first step into the office.

The light was plentiful, even dazzling, but it fell upon decor that stopped me dead in my tracks. I felt a strong blast of territorial repulse, which overpowered by many degrees of magnitude the faint breeze of my official permission to enter. Everything about this office screamed *"not mine."* There were pictures of kittens nestled in bow-bedecked baskets; there were actual bow-bedecked baskets filled with teensy-weensy dried flowers. There were cherubs and hearts in two and three dimensions. The relentless buttons-and-bows motif of the office took me by surprise, because I knew its resident only by her poetry, which is sometimes sly and feline but never coy or kittenish. Whatever those totems of hypertonic femininity meant to her, they seemed toxic to me.

Entering that office, I felt as if I had stumbled upon storybook doll headquarters—the command center where my mother and aunts plotted how to get me out of flannel-lined, size-6 jeans and into ruffled pinafores; where they swapped my beloved doctor's kit for an uncoveted nurse's; and where, many years later, they hid my pilfered copy of James Baldwin's *Another Country* after stealing glimpses of its steamy first page. My Iowa aunts were not actually present for these treacheries, which transpired in Illinois, but they hovered in spirit over the perfumed backroom of maternal conniving, psychically urging my mother to keep my innocence as unstained as my white satin baby shoes, preserved to this day in their cottony coffin.

Like most mothers, mine wanted to keep me safe from mud and scars and sin; perhaps more than most daughters, I preferred to take my lumps. With the help of my father and changing times and my mother's own deep ambivalence about her role as social enforcer, I won most of those early battles. I must have felt, however, that the stakes were high and the calls close, because the cloying atmosphere of the poet's office, like the potpourried air of certain gift-shop shrines to the itsy-bitsy, can still inspire a fear of suffocation.

Without a moment's hesitation, I returned to my own dark office and began to think—not about the poet, or what possessed her to decorate as she did, and not about my many skirmishes in the on-going gender wars, but about the territorial impulse and what stimulates it in me. To the extent that I had given thought to this matter, which was slight, I think I had confused the territorial with the proprietorial impulse, which stakes out a straightforward claim of "It's mine, stay away from it, I bought it, paid for it, and you can't play with it, drive it, wear it, sleep in it, or eat it." I exercise my proprietary rights as much as the next person, and respect them in others. But that was not the force that had virtually blown me out of the poet's office; after all, I had been graciously invited to enter. And although the poet had marked her room as assiduously as any cat, it wasn't the markings per se that stopped me, but the *ad feminam* aura of threat emanating from them, as if they were encoded with a message decipherable only by me: "All hope abandon, ye who enter here."

That an aura of threat should trigger a strong territorial *repulse* in me was no great revelation, except that it implied its opposite: My territorial *impulses* must be triggered by places that emanate an aura of safety and bear an encoded message of hope. I knew very well what those places were, but I hadn't thought about them in those terms. My home is my locus of self-constructed safety, but I feel less territorial (as opposed to proprietorial) about my home than I do about the county in which it is situated. And if there was one word I most routinely associated with the county, it was not safety, but beauty.

From the day I first drove through Columbia County, on a serendipitous detour from Vermont to Manhattan, I knew I wanted to live there someday. The house I bought eight years later was the affordable means to that end, and as attached as I have become to it, the house is replaceable; the county is not. Like most people who live in Columbia County, I take a strong provincial pride in the beauty of its rural landscape, but upon reflection I realized that if beauty were the sole source of my attachment, I would not experience what I do when I drive south from my home in Ancram along County Route 7.

In the parlance of travel brochures, Columbia County is a rural area of upstate New York known for its gorgeous rolling farmland, its meandering trout streams, and its breathtaking vistas of distant mountain ranges to the east and west. Columbia County happens to share its southern border and its views of distant mountains with equally beautiful, equally rolling, and equally stream-laced northern Dutchess County. On the map, the line dividing the two counties is straight, but the road closest to the county line, like the terrain it winds through, is curved and hilly. So as I drive, for instance, along a certain stretch of County Route 7, I am in fact crisscrossing the invisible border every several hundred yards or so.

Most of the crossings are unmarked, and so I remain happily oblivious to the jurisdictional realities that press upon the herds of dairy cows I gaze upon. But every so often, there is a small green sign saying WELCOME TO DUTCHESS COUNTY, followed, a curve or two later, by a sign welcoming me back to Columbia County, followed a curve or two . . . well, you see the pattern. Each time these signs reach my consciousness, something just a hair's breadth below that level whispers, Theirs . . . Mine . . . Theirs . . . well, you see the pattern. The strange thing is, that nagging little whisper actually changes how I feel about what I'm seeing out my car window from curve to curve. Inflate, deflate, expand, contract, embrace, resist. Little flares of county pride and county spite. Driving country roads, usually so soothing, becomes emotionally exhausting.

If both counties are indistinguishably beautiful, particularly along their shared border, why is my response to the sight of their splendors so different? When I asked myself that question in the wake of my retreat from the poet's office, the answer rose to the surface like a bubble of gas from the disturbed bottom of a pond. The welcome extended by the cows on the Columbia County side of the border reaches farther, spreading through the many square miles of dairy farms that have kept some families here for eight generations. South of the border, the cows are a thin veneer, like the iconic painted Guernseys of quaint country decor. Crossing that border brings you one county closer to Manhattan, whose colonizing wealth has turned cow country into horse country, a province of tax shelters and hunt clubs. I have nothing against horses, but Dutchess County horse farms bring to mind Thoreau's maxim, "Beware of all enterprises that require new clothes."

In fact, the economic divide between counties is becoming blurred as the reach of the city creeps northward, but for reasons of my own, I draw a clear line on my mental map, which transforms the curves of County Route 7 into a series of dangerous border crossings. In my cartography, safety lies to the north, in cow country, safety from the presumptions and pretensions of extravagant wealth, from the pull of obsessive careerism and urban fetishism, from the bridle of competitive consumption and display—safety, in short, from the necessity of new clothes. In cow country, I can regard as formal attire any article of apparel not worn in the creek more than once. Its beauty is an affordable beauty, which made possible my purchase of the greatest luxuries of all, time to fill as I wish, the solitude to create my days from scratch, to bestow my attention wherever it is naturally drawn. This was the hope I saw in the hills when I first drove through Columbia County in a previous life of seventy-hour work weeks.

Beauty, safety, hope. I am always aware first of the beauty and only later, if at all, of what it holds for me. This is true on many levels, but I am speaking now of landscape and in particular of Winchell Mountain, to which I attach my strongest territorial feeling. The plateau on top of Winchell Mountain is the highest terrain I traverse in the routine conduct of my life, and it offers the most sweeping views. The eye moves unobstructed over the lush green Hudson Valley to the sharp profile of Catskill peaks ranging high across the west, and to the rounded summits of the Berkshires nestled one behind another like an infinite progression of blue moons rising in the east. Once, at the end of a short, gray winter's day, I stood on top of Winchell Mountain looking west toward a pool of turquoise light lapping against a neon orange sky, which transformed slowly into a luminous chartreuse lake overflowing magenta banks. My father later said the rare palette of that sunset must have been painted by ice crystals in the air.

Like most people in Ancram, I go over Winchell Mountain several times a week to reach the nearest supermarket, movie theater, bookstore. Driving up the mountain from home, I am in Columbia County; driving down the other side, I am in Dutchess County. Somewhere along its plateau, I cross an unmarked border, but I pay it no mind. I regard the plateau as no-man's-land, even though it is tilled by the Pulver family, whose vastly understated claim is staked by a sign that reads "Pleasant View Farm." I am not alone in this feeling. Even the most prosaic people I know become poets when they cross Winchell Mountain, swept up like Emerson in transcendental sentiment about New England farmland: "The charming landscape which I saw this morning is indubitably made up of some twenty or thirty farms. Miller owns this field, Locke that, and Manning the woodland beyond. But none of them owns the landscape. There is a property in the horizon which no man has but he whose eye can integrate all the parts, that is, the poet."

I imagine that for almost everyone there is a landscape that inspires a sense of the transcendent, that meets what

Thoreau called "our need to witness our limits transgressed."
It is not necessarily the landscape that is ancestrally or personally familiar, or that evokes the greatest awe. I have
stood, camera round my neck, on the rim of the Grand
Canyon; I have felt the spray of the ocean surf pounding
against outcroppings of rock in Baja, Maine, and Big Sur. I
have nestled my back against the sun-warmed rock of pre-
historic cliff dwellings in the American Southwest. I have
stood on the slight rise of a cemetery in central Iowa where
my great-grandmother is buried—a slight rise and yet so
much higher than the surrounding flatness that I could see
for miles to the next rise, on which sat the next cemetery,
where her husband, divided from her in death by religion, is
buried. All these places inspired awe, a consciousness of
privilege to have witnessed their manifest or quiet grandeur.
But it was Winchell Mountain that met my need to witness
my limits transgressed.

There is an emotion I have come to call "the feeling of
enormity." I first felt it when I was driving along County
Route 7 one Sunday afternoon in August 1992, shortly after
Hurricane Andrew had wreaked devastation on southern
Florida. I had seen televised images of survivors, their eyes
still glazed with shock, wandering amid the rubble of their
former lives, hunting for any small shard of what had been
theirs, as if such talismans might contain the meaning or the
magic to restore them to their innocence. Driving with
those images still vivid in my mind's eye, I saw, as if in a waking dream, the ghost of myself walking alone and uncom-
prehending through a broken landscape of wreckage. I knew
at once that my personal hurricane, long forecast, had finally

hit. Faint and nauseous, I slowed and pulled over to the side of the road.

For the first time, I felt the full impact of what I had become—the lone survivor of a natural disaster wandering in the wasteland of my family's destruction. Until that moment, I had experienced their trials and mine as a sequence: My mother had fought death tooth and nail, as if it were the angel of hell on earth, and when at last she was overpowered, I felt not only loss but also the staggering sadness of her defeat. Along the way, something had also been gained—the drawing together of my father and myself in our care for her. When my father died two years later, it was a graceful surrender, like Lee at Appomattox, and I missed most what he had become to me at the end of our life together. The gain this time was the drawing together of my brother and myself in our care for him. Three years later, when my brother, a doctor to his last gasp, met death as if reluctantly bowing to his new chief of staff, I raged for him. And then I became numb, stupefied by what I had witnessed over these six years—my mother's long wasting, my brother's slow suffocation, the skin stripped from my father's body by disease, leaving him swaddled in bandages like the burned victim of an atomic blast.

Before the numbness set in, I had become used to regular visitation by certain emotions, grief, anger, pity, and what I called "the fish hook"—the quick puncture and deflation of my errant impulses toward joy. I might feel, for instance, a reflexive burst of pleasure at waking to a beautiful day, then be reeled abruptly back to sadness by the knowledge that the day was not theirs to enjoy. Routinely waylaid, I had struggled to accept their sufferings, and deaths, one by one, but there was a trauma to the totality separate from each of the losses, and ten months after the last death, I still had not reckoned with its force.

Now roused from my stupor by the televised spectacle of Hurricane Andrew's unsparing violence, I felt a terror so overwhelming that it literally drove me off the road. The closest I can come to conveying "the feeling of enormity" is to say it is the cosmic paranoia of feeling singled out for a trial beyond one's strength by a force incomparably larger and more implacable than one's self. It's the kind of feeling that makes one ask, "Why me?" The emotion took my breath away, sickened me, and when I had recovered enough to continue driving, I sped toward the safety of home as if from a dark and glowering sky. But the safety I sought was not there; the protection its walls offered felt as puny as I did in comparison to the forces arrayed against me.

The emotion did not take up permanent residence in me, but made unpredictable, battering appearances through-out the remainder of that summer. Then one night in early October it descended upon me as I happened to be return-ing alone from the movie theater, driving up the steep slope of Winchell Mountain at midnight on a clear, moonlit night. I kept driving, praying for enough composure to cross the plateau and begin the long coast downhill toward home. But halfway across the plateau, some instinct urged me to stop. Better my breath be taken by beauty than by fear. I parked my car on the shoulder and walked back down the road to the rise of the old Winchell family cemetery, and on past those slanting slabs of slate into a cornfield in search of the

absolute highest square foot on the mountain. I thought that
if I could plant my feet there, on the top of my world, and
swivel round until I had taken in all 360 degrees, the feeling
of enormity might lift from me.

As I wandered at midnight over the broken stalks of a
recent harvest, seeking the elusive high ground, I became
more and more fixed upon that moonlit view from the summit as my last, best hope for safety. I moved from rise to rise,
each seeming to promise a more comprehensive view, only to
find my line of sight blocked by a stand of trees in one direction or an unharvested field in another. Finally, in despair of
finding the perfect vantage, I stopped walking and looked up
at the sky. Full and high in the west, the moon cast enough
light for the Catskills to rise in distant silhouette and, nearer,
to bestow a golden shimmer on the stubbled fields.

I didn't need the 360-degree view, this perspective
was enough. I stood still, letting the moon shine indiffer-
ently on me, and I knew with perfect clarity that I had not
been singled out. I was simply part of the landscape, part
of what is living, which is also part of what is dying. I felt
very small, and very free. I had shed the last remnants of a
fortunate child's innocence, the persistent illusion of cen-
trality, but I had gained my place in the universe. It might
seem cold comfort, to find solace in the moonglow of an
indifferent universe, but the release from singularity felt
like salvation to me.

As I walked back to my car, taking deep breaths of the
chilly night air, I became aware of a half-submerged refrain
that had been trying to raise itself to consciousness all the
while I had been wandering from rise to rise. Now it surfaced,

mantralike and mystifying: "Em-ped-o-cles, Em-ped-o-cles." Where on earth did that come from? Under the pressure of its metered beat, I searched my memory and came up with a poem: "Empedocles on Etna," by Matthew Arnold. I had read it for an English survey class when I was nineteen years old, and though I vaguely remembered its having a great impact on me at the time, I no longer remembered why. In fact, after almost thirty years, I was able to retrieve nothing from wherever it is we catalogue lost knowledge beyond its title and author.

Home again, I rummaged through my bookshelves until I found the poem, but seeing it was long and the hour late, I left it for another day. When I returned the next morning to *Masters of British Literature*, Volume Two, page 719, I found the poem, first published in 1853, yellowed not with age but with indelible Magic Marker. So many veins of transparent gold ran through the text, it seems I must have hung on every word at nineteen, not prescient enough in 1964 to question the wisdom of dead white males.

Arnold's apparent alter ego in this dramatic poem is the poet-philosopher Empedocles, who, "half-mad with exile and brooding on his wrongs," climbs to the glowing summit of Mount Etna on a starlit fifth-century B.C. night, hoping to find a cure there for "his settled gloom."

Alone, weary, and "dead to every natural joy," disdainful of fools who invent "Harsh Gods and hostile Fates" to blame for "ills we ought to bear," Empedocles looks to the "cold-shining lights" brilliant above him for any slight beacon of hope. And he finds, at last, not only comfort but elation, in the knowledge that, though he may not have lived well or joyously, he has "Sophisticated no truth,/Nursed no delusion,/Allow'd no fear." Released from despair by stoic acceptance of his human lot, Empedocles is exultant: "The numbing cloud/Mounts off my soul, I feel it, I breathe free." But then, before his soaring spirit flags, as he fears it must, he plunges into the crater, hoping to seal his soul forever in the moment of his exaltation.

Matthew Arnold eventually rejected "Empedocles," banishing the poem from a later collection, but *not*, he explained, "because the subject of it was a Sicilian Greek born between two and three thousand years ago, although many persons would think this a sufficient reason." In retrospect, he thought his depiction of Empedocles' "mental distress" was "accurate" but "morbid," because his pain was too prolonged and unrelieved. And there was, in Arnold's mind, no justification for poetry that did not "inspirit and rejoice the reader."

Arnold judged himself and Empedocles too harshly. At nineteen, I saw no necessity, nor do I now, to plunge either the poem or the ancient Greek into the crater of oblivion. What "inspirited" me then, apparently so forcefully that it could draw me all unwitting onto Winchell Mountain at midnight thirty years later, was the revelation that there was a deep satisfaction in living without illusions. Whether of a divinely ordered universe, or of a humanly attainable 360-degree view. Empedocles found relief on the summit, and so did I. I needed to be reminded that, no matter how high the summit, I might win "a thousand glimpses" but never see the whole. I needed to be reminded that, for better or worse, I'm just part of the setting.

I know that it seems strange to some, including some of those closest to me, that I find comfort where I do. Alone at midnight on a moonlit mountaintop. Swimming stroke after stroke through glassy water. Some ask, and others look as if they want to ask, why I do not look for comfort in the company of other loving humans. The answer is that I have and do look to love and friendship. I am not a misanthrope, nor a recluse, although these past ten years have been far more solitary than previous decades of my life. They have been years of my coming to terms with a certain irreducible degree of aloneness, which I think I've always believed is part of the human lot but which I have apprehended more deeply in the wake of my family's death.

It is not that I found other human beings wanting, but that I found them, like me, mortal, which is, I guess, a kind of profound unreliability. So I searched in these years for other sources of reassurance, and the wonder is, I found so many of them, and in such unpredictable places. Dreams, memories, all-consuming physical exertion, newly acquired knowledge, and shards of long-forgotten learning retrieved to serve a new purpose; a stray fact about butterfly migrations, a poem about a dead Greek. All these came to my rescue. But above all, I found comfort in no-man's-land, in those landscapes whose open horizons induce a larger perspective.

I have become intensely territorial about certain patches of earth, not because I think they are mine, but because I think they are no one's, and whoever would stake an exclusive claim to them violates me and something much larger than me. Not too long ago, driving across the plateau of Winchell Mountain, I saw a large new sign, advertising twenty-six lots for "luxury home sites." I felt rage, and fanta-sized returning under cover of dark with a chainsaw. That night I had this dream:

It was midnight, and I was standing with a group of friends on a hilltop near the Arctic Circle, where I hoped to see the aurora borealis for the first time in my life. I looked up and the light show was starting. The stars were dancing, not streaking across wide distances like shooting stars, but dancing in place, creating a quick constant flickering that could almost be mistaken for the blurred view of a bright sta-tionary object. At first I was disappointed, because I had expected to see streams of colored light rushing through the night sky, but the longer I watched the dancing stars, the more amazing the sight became to me, and gradually I understood that the stars were telling the story of the uni-verse, their flickering a signal encoded with all the truth and wisdom that is.

I looked to my right, toward the others, to see if they were experiencing what I was, and I saw, high in another section of sky, an astounding sight—an edifice, monumental in scale and fascist in style, like a Third Reich government building as it might have been filmed by Leni Riefenstahl. Debris was crashing into the building, falling from higher in the sky, as if drawn to it by magnetic force. Broken airplane wings and fuselages, old weather balloons, twisted bits of exploded spy satellites, all the remains of what men had sent into the sky over these last decades. The building was a celestial landfill. When I tried to draw the others' attention from the dancing stars to this building, I realized that no one else could see it. I tried fruitlessly to raise an alarm, not that the sky was falling, but that it was being marked, claimed as a colony for the few. Wreckage was blotting out not just the horizon but all of space.

I awoke, and was relieved. It was just a nightmare. There is debris in outer space, and a building. But there are other open horizons, only light years away.

A c k n o w l e d g m e n t s

I WOULD LIKE TO THANK Martha Norton, whose skills as midwife to memory helped make this book possible; my students, whose dedication to writing inspires my own; my neighbor Betty Hamilton, whose generous permission to roam her lands saved me from a life of criminal trespass; Nick Lyons, the kind of publisher writers more often dream of than encounter. Above all, I thank Milena Herring, whose unfailingly sound instincts and advice contributed immeasurably both to the living and the writing of this book.